D0735836

Committed to Christ
and His Church

Books in the Stephen F. Olford Biblical Preaching Library

Committed to Christ and His Church

Preaching on Discipleship and Membership

Stephen F. Olford

BAKER BOOK HOUSE
Grand Rapids, Michigan 49516

Copyright 1991 by
Baker Book House Company

ISBN: 0-8010-6717-0

Third printing, November 1992

Printed in the United States of America

These resources were adapted from material published by the Institute for
Biblical Preaching, volume 5—2, 3, 4, Box 757800, Memphis, TN 38175-7800.

The New King James Version is used as the basis for this Bible study. Occasion-
ally the King James Version (KJV) is used.

The author is grateful to the many copyright owners for the use of their material.

Contents

Introduction

The priority program on heaven's agenda is the calling out and completion of the church, the body of Christ. When Jesus declared, ". . . I will build my church, and the gates of Hades shall not prevail against it" (Matt. 16:18), he launched a movement that no devil in hell or angel in heaven can ever thwart. Notwithstanding its many failures and factions, the true church of redeemed and regenerated souls will prevail. One day soon she will be raptured and presented before the presence of the Savior himself ". . . a glorious church, not having spot or wrinkle or any such thing . . ." (Eph. 5:27).

It follows, therefore, that our main task as pastors, teachers, and leaders is to ". . . [warn] every man and [teach] every man in all wisdom, that we may present every man perfect in Christ Jesus" (Col. 1:28). To this end we need to give ourselves to a church-family ministry.

This third volume of the Stephen Olford Biblical Preaching Library focuses on this "family ministry." We start with a series on "The Demands of Discipleship." This is an in-depth examination of New Testament discipleship. One reason we are witnessing such defections from our local churches today is because we have forgotten the demands of discipleship in our ministry of follow-up.

This leads quite naturally to another series on "God's Blueprint for Church Membership." These sermon/lectures contain material I consistently used in our membership classes in all the churches I served. No one received "the right hand of fellowship" without attending each class and signing the Covenant of Membership (before an elder board) at the conclusion of the stated number of weeks.

As you expand and expound these sermon outlines, make sure that you preach ". . . in demonstration of the Spirit and of power, that [the faith of your people] should not be in the wisdom of men but in the power of God" (1 Cor. 2:4–5).

So I exhort you to "preach the word. . . . do the work of an evangelist, [and] make full proof of [your] ministry" (2 Tim. 4:2, 5, KJV). God richly bless you!

Stephen F. Olford

Part 1

The Demands
of Discipleship

1

The Disciple's Relationship
Matthew 10:16–27;
Luke 6:35–42; John 13:1–17

"A disciple is not above his teacher, but everyone who is perfectly trained will be like his teacher" (Luke 6:40).

Introduction

The term *disciple* is used consistently in the four gospels to describe the relationship between Christ and his followers. Jesus used it in speaking of them, and they employed it when referring to one another. The term did not pass out of use in the days following Pentecost; on the contrary, the word runs throughout the Acts of the Apostles (see 9:1, 26; 20:7, 30; 21:16). In fact, the members of the early church were known as disciples before they were first called "Christians" at Antioch (see Acts 11:26). The word signifies "a taught or trained one." Jesus is the teacher and we are the learners. He has all knowledge of the ultimate purposes of God for us, and we are the seekers after truth. As a teacher, the Lord Jesus is not merely a lecturer, from whose dissertations we may deduce certain lessons; nor, indeed, is he only a prophet who delivers his burden and then leaves us with the issues. Rather, he is the teacher who bends over his pupils with the set purpose of training them step by step, until they become identified with the teacher himself. The gospels teach that:

I. The Disciple Is One Who Is Identified with the Master's Discipline

"A disciple is not above his teacher, nor a servant above his master" (10:24; see also vv. 16–27). The context shows that the Lord Jesus had been misunderstood and misinterpreted, and he warns his disciples that they would suffer in a similar manner since the disciple is not above his master, nor the servant above his Lord. As a son, Jesus Christ ". . . learned obedience by the things which he suffered" (Heb. 5:8); and in this regard we must follow in his steps. The greatest privilege you and I can have is to be identified with the master in his discipline. Such discipline will be one of:

A. Personal Persecution

". . . you will be hated by all for my name's sake . . ." (10:22). No one can be a genuine disciple without encountering some form of personal persecution. Jesus promised this: ". . . If they persecuted me, they will also persecute you . . ." (John 15:20). In the face of such persecution, however, the Lord Jesus promises *the power of utterance:* ". . . do not worry about how or what you should speak. For it will be given to you in that hour what you should speak" (Matt. 10:19).

Under the fires of persecution, one of the greatest disciplines is that of controlling our thoughts, tempers, and tongues. Left to our own resources, we should fail miserably and bring dishonor to the name of our Lord. This is where the master promises the power of the Holy Spirit to control thoughts, tempers, and tongues. How wonderfully this was illustrated in the master's life—particularly when he suffered under Pontius Pilate. *What discipline of speech and silence he exercised on that momentous occasion!* No wonder the apostle Paul uses this event in the experience of our Lord as the basis of his call to a life of discipline and control. Note his words to Timothy: "I urge you in the sight of God who gives life to all things, and before *Christ Jesus who witnessed the good confession before Pontius Pilate,* that you keep this commandment without spot, blameless until our Lord Jesus Christ's appearing" (1 Tim. 6:13–14).

Under the pressure of persecution, the Lord Jesus also promises *the power of endurance–* ". . . he who endures to the end will be saved" (10:22). The patience and longsuffering required at times like this are only possible when the believer knows the discipline of the master in his life. It was said of the Savior that ". . . for the joy that was set before him [he] endured the cross, despising the shame, and has sat down at the right hand of the throne of God" (Heb. 12:2).

Illustration

The following incident is related by Mrs. Charles Spurgeon, who suffered greatly for more than a quarter of a century: "At the close of a gloomy day I lay resting on my couch as night drew on. Though all was bright within my cozy room, some of the external darkness seemed to enter my soul and obscure its spiritual vision. In sorrow of heart I asked, 'Why does my Lord deal thus with his child? Why does he permit lingering weakness to hinder the sweet service I long to render to his servants?'" For awhile silence reigned in the little room, broken only by the crackling of the oak log burning in the fireplace. Suddenly she heard a sweet, soft sound, a little clear musical note like the tender trill of a robin, and wondered what it could be. Surely, no bird would be singing outside at that time of the year and night. Suddenly she realized it was coming from the log on the fire; the fire was letting loose the imprisoned music from the old oak's inmost heart. Perhaps the tree had garnered up this song in the days when all was well, when birds twittered merrily on its branches, and sunlight decked the tender leaves with gold. Mrs. Spurgeon thought, "When the fire of affliction draws songs of praise from us, then we are truly purified and God is glorified." As she mused on this her soul found comfort. Singing in the fire! If that is the only way for God to get harmony out of these hard, apathetic hearts, then let the furnace be heated seven times hotter than before![1]

B. Spiritual Opposition

"If they have called the master of the house Beelzebub, how much more will they call those of his household!" (10:25). Spiritual opposition is the deliberate failure to rightly understand and interpret the work of God. Such opposition often tends to distress and depress the disciple, but Jesus reassures his own by telling them: ". . . do not fear them. For there is nothing covered that will not be revealed, and hidden that will not be known" (10:26). The Savior says that however unjustly we may be opposed by misunderstanding and misinterpretation, there is going to be a day of disclosure and vindication. Our business is to press on regardlessly, speaking in the light what God has taught us in the darkness of persecution and opposition; preaching from the housetops what he has whispered to us in the time of discipline.

We must learn that if we would rise to the measure of true discipleship we must count it a joy to suffer for Christ. It is recorded of those early disciples that after persecution and opposition ". . . they departed from the presence of the council, rejoicing that they were counted worthy to suffer shame for his name" (Acts 5:41). God gives us the grace to be willing to suffer likewise. Only thus shall we know a true identification with the master's discipline.

Illustration

Adoniram Judson, the renowned missionary to Burma, endured untold hardships trying to reach the lost for Christ. For seven heartbreaking years he suffered hunger and privation. During this time he was thrown into Ava Prison, and for seventeen months was subjected to almost incredible mistreatment. As a result, for the rest of his life he carried the ugly marks made by the chains and iron shackles which had cruelly bound him. Undaunted, upon his release, he asked for permission to enter another province where he might resume preaching the gospel. The godless ruler indignantly denied his request, saying, "My people are not fools enough to listen to anything a missionary might say, but I fear they might be impressed by your scars and turn to your religion!"

II. The Disciple Is One Who Is Identified with the Master's Discernment

"A disciple is not above his teacher, but everyone who is perfectly trained will be like his teacher" (Luke 6:40; see also vv. 35–42). A consideration of this portion reveals that there are two elements in this discernment:

A. The Maturity of Knowledge

"A disciple is not above his teacher, but everyone who is perfectly trained [or made mature in knowledge] will be like his teacher" (6:40). Our Lord had just quoted a well-known proverbial parable: ". . . Can the blind lead the blind? Will they not both fall into the ditch?" (6:39). Virtually he was saying that the blind cannot lead the blind, any better than the blind man can guide himself; the inference being that until a man is perfect, he will abstain from needless, hasty, and uncharitable judgment of others.

The purpose of the master teacher is to develop his disciple in knowledge, both academically and experimentally. Only by such perfection of knowledge can the disciple be identified with the master's discernment. It was with this thought in mind that Jesus said, "A disciple is not above his teacher, but everyone who is perfectly trained will be like his teacher" (6:40).

Illustration

Peter Waldo, the probable leader of the pious Waldensians, was a rich merchant of Lyons, France. He was converted through the death of a friend at a feast. He then had the Scriptures translated by two erudite scholars into his own tongue, and thereafter gave up all his wealth and followed his Lord. Everywhere he went he preached the claims of Christ, using the words "Look to Jesus! Listen to Jesus! Learn of Jesus!" These are the prerequisites of discipleship.[2]

B. The Authority of Judgment

". . . why do you look at the speck in your brother's eye, but do not perceive the plank in your own eye?" (6:41). The principle the Savior is teaching here is that what we judge in others is invariably what we are guilty of ourselves. We see the speck (splinter) in our brother's eye, but forget that we are even more blind because of a plank in our own eyes.

Illustration

A lady in Switzerland brought a small package of greatly aged cheese. Putting it in her handbag, she continued her shopping in different stores. She was greatly repelled at what she thought was the malodor of the different clerks encountered. Her thoughts ran something like this: "How can these illsmelling clerks maintain their positions?" Imagine her embarrassment when opening her handbag to discover that it was she, not others, who was responsible for the offensive odor![3]

Judgment, born of the maturity of knowledge, must be characterized by:

1. CAUTIOUSNESS

"Judge not, and you shall not be judged. Condemn not, and you shall not be condemned. Forgive, and you will be forgiven" (6:37). An evidence of immaturity is hasty judgment and destructive criticism. Authoritative judgment, on the other hand, will be marked by a cautiousness which withholds condemnation until the possibility of forgiveness is thoroughly explored. The fact that we are not to condemn, but to forgive, does not mean that we are not to judge; that would be a contradiction of Scripture. The warning, rather, is that of cautiousness and constructiveness in judgment.

2. GRACIOUSNESS

". . . be merciful, just as your Father also is merciful" (6:36). Authoritative judgment is always tempered with grace. The goodness and severity of God are not at variance. This is why the psalmist could say, "I will sing of mercy and justice . . ." (Ps. 101:1); and the prophet could say: ". . . In wrath remember mercy" (Hab. 3:2).

3. BOUNTEOUSNESS

"Give, and it will be given to you: good measure, pressed down, shaken together, and running over will be put into your bosom. For with the same measure that you use, it will be measured back to you" (6:38). With the cautiousness and graciousness, there must be a bounteousness in judgment. If graciousness speaks of largeheartedness, then bounteousness is a token of largemindedness. This is the kind of authoritative judgment which takes all relevant facts into account. Someone has defined wisdom as "the right application of knowledge to any given situation in the light of all the verified facts." Such wisdom is bounteous judgment. Phillip Brooks once prayed, "Let me not lose faith in my fellow men. Keep me sweet and sound of heart, in spite of ingratitude, treachery or meanness. Preserve me from minding little stings or giving them." What a rare grace this is today!

III. The Disciple Is One Who Is Identified with the Master's Devotedness

". . . I have given you an example, that you should do as I have done to you. Most assuredly, I say to you, a servant is not greater than his master; nor is he who is sent greater than he who sent him" (John 13:15–16 see also vv. 1–17). An examination of the context reveals that Jesus had just performed an act of superlative selflessness—that of washing the disciples' feet. Although this act of devoted service was performed hours before the agony of Gethsemane, the cruelty of the cross, and the desertion of his disciples, the Savior refused to be deflected from humbling himself to attend to the needs of his unworthy disciples. How easy it is to be taken up with our own sufferings or successes and so become self-centered or indifferent to the needs of others. As far as our Lord was concerned, however, his devotedness was complete. Consider:

A. The Reality of Such Devotedness

"Jesus . . . rose from supper and laid aside his garments, took a towel and girded himself. After that, he poured water into a basin and began to wash the disciples' feet, and to wipe them with the towel with which he was girded" (13:4–5). To wash the feet of guests at a feast was the work of a slave; but notwithstanding this he willingly made himself a bondslave, ". . . taking the form of a servant . . ." (Phil. 2:7). This reality of devotedness to "slave" for others was characteristic of the Savior throughout his ministry. He could say, ". . . the Son of Man did not come to be served, but to serve, and to give his life a ransom for many" (Matt. 20:28).

Illustration

A young woman who had left home because of her drunken father later became a Christian. Thereafter she announced her intention of returning and doing what she could to reclaim him. "But what will you do when he finds fault with all your efforts to please him?" someone asked. "Try a little harder," she answered with a light in her eyes. "Yes, but when he is unreasonable and unkind you will be tempted to lose your temper, and answer him angrily. What will you do then?" "Pray a little harder," came the answer. The discourager had one more arrow: "Suppose he should strike you as he did before. What could you do but leave him again?" "Love him a little harder," said the young Christian steadily. Her splendid perseverance conquered. Through love, prayer, and patient effort, her father was not only reclaimed from his besetting sin, but proved Christ's power to save. To what extent are we identified with this characteristic in our devotedness?[4]

B. The Morality of Such Devotedness

Having lovingly, voluntarily, and perfectly washed his disciples' feet, Jesus said to them, ". . . I have given you an example, that you should do as I have done to you. Most assuredly, I say to you, a servant is not greater than his master; nor is he who is sent greater than he who sent him" (13:15–16). Christ supremely demonstrates the devotedness of a disciplined life. He calls us to demonstrate a quality of life so that those who follow us will emulate the example of Christ. To what extent are others led into a life of devotedness because of what they see in us?

Illustration

When Catherine Booth, "Mother of the Salvation Army" died in 1890 of cancer, her body lay in state in Congress Hall. The poorest of the poor mingled with members of Parliament as they filed past the casket; all were eager for a last look upon the face they loved. Ruffians passed her weeping. Prostitutes turned from her side and begged to be taken to some home where they could begin a new life. "That woman lived for me," an alcoholic cried in anguish. They drew him aside, and down on his knees he accepted pardon and promised that her God should be his. Three men knelt together one night at the head of the coffin, repented of their sins, and left the hall saved. Another said, "I've come sixty miles to see her again. She was the means of saving my two boys." What a thrilling testimony to one who had exemplified the qualities of a Christian![5]

Conclusion

The three experiences which perfect our relationship as disciples are identification with Christ in his discipline, discernment, and devotedness. Such identification matures only as we daily bring our lives under the mastership of his personal tuition. So may our prayer ever be:

> At the feet of Jesus
> Is the place for me;
> There, a humble learner,
> I would choose to be.
>   P. P. Bliss

2

The Disciple's Responsibility

John 8:31–36

"If you abide in my word, you are my disciples indeed.
And you shall know the truth, and the truth shall make
you free" (8:31–32).

Introduction

When the right relationship has been established in the
School of Discipline, there is a lifelong responsibility
which emerges for every true disciple of Jesus Christ. It is
comprehended in the words of our text: ". . . If you abide
in my word, you are my disciples indeed. And you shall
know the truth, and the truth shall make you free"
(8:31–32). The disciple's responsibility must be regarded as
threefold:

I. Continuance in the Word of Truth

". . . If *you* abide in my word . . ." (8:31). The emphasis is on the pronoun "you." This is significant because

the Lord Jesus was addressing leaders of religious life who were nominal believers—men who did not possess the conviction or courage to rank themselves openly as the disciples of Christ. True discipleship demands:

A. Continuance in the Truth as it Is in Christ

He had just said, ". . . Even if I bear witness of myself, my witness is true . . ." (8:14). The Jews required the testimony of two witnesses before they accepted a record as valid. This requirement was based on the imperfection of individual knowledge and the untrustworthiness of individual testimony. With Christ, however, there was no imperfection or untrustworthiness. So as to give men no excuse to doubt his Word he declared, "I am One who bears witness of me" (8:18). In other words, he claimed to represent the two required witnesses since he was one with the Father in *speaking,* as well as *being,* the truth. To grasp such a claim is to be willing to continue in the truth as it is in Jesus Christ.

B. Continuance in the Whole Truth as it Is in Christ

". . . If you abide in my word . . ." (8:31). Notice that the Lord speaks of "my word" in the singular. In Chapter 15:7 we have the opposite form of the thought where he says, "If you abide in me, and my words abide in you . . ." The reason for the singular form in this context is that Christ was demanding continuance in the truth in its entirety from would-be disciples. By the term *my word,* Jesus was conveying the idea of the full revelation of God as it is in himself. It is easy to be selective in our loyalty to truth, but such selectiveness is not worthy of discipleship.

Illustration

When bankers are trained to learn the difference between a counterfeit bill and a real one they are told not to waste time studying the counterfeit; they study the real thing until they know it upside down, backwards and forwards. Then when a counterfeit bill comes along it stands out like a sore thumb. In like manner, we must study the real thing—Christ and his life. Only then shall we continue in the truth.

C. Continuance in Nothing but the Truth as it Is in Christ

". . . If you abide in my word . . ." (8:31). The human tendency is to cease to "abide" in the Word, and to be led astray by our own opinions and preconceived ideas. We must ever remember that truth is the objective apprehension of the revelation of Christ, as distinguished from human speculations distorted by desires and special interests. To continue in the truth, the whole truth, and nothing but the truth, is to be guided wholly by the Word of God and governed wholly by the Spirit of God in all matters of faith and practice. This constitutes true discipleship.

> Since truth is always true
> And only true can be,
> Keep me, O Lord, as true to truth
> As truth is true to Thee.[1]
> T. Baird

II. Obedience to the Word of Truth

"And you shall *know* the truth . . ." (8:32). The Lord Jesus left men in no doubt as to what he meant by knowing the truth. In this very gospel he says, "If anyone wants to do [God's] will, he shall know concerning the doctrine, whether it is from God . . ." (John 7:17). Willingness to do God's will is the secret of progressive knowledge in divine things. Someone has put it:

> Light obeyed bringeth light;
> Light rejected bringeth night.

A. There Must Be Obedience of Mind

Paul speaks of ". . . bringing every thought into captivity to the obedience of Christ" (2 Cor. 10:5). This calls for the casting down of our own carnal imaginations and proud rationalizations so that the Word of God may dwell in us richly in all wisdom. In terms of practical experience, this involves reading the Bible every day. Repeatedly, the master had to turn to his disciples and ask, ". . . Have you not read . . .?" (Matt. 12:3; see also 19:4; 21:16; 22:31, etc.). The apostle Paul exhorted Timothy to ". . . give attention to reading . . ." (1 Tim. 4:13). More than just the public reading of Scripture, Paul was concerned that Timothy might become neglectful of this holy habit in his personal life. As martyrdom drew perilously near, that apostle admonished Timothy again: "Be diligent to come to me quickly; . . . [and] Bring . . . the books, *especially the parchments*" (2 Tim. 4:9, 13). Think of it! Here Paul was in prison. Death was near, heaven was soon to open to receive him, but this man of God felt the need for more reading, especially the parchments—the Holy Scriptures. What an indictment on our reading of the Word in these days of rushed living.

But along with the reading there should be the searching of the Word of God every day. ". . . search the Scriptures," said our Lord to the religious leaders of his day, "for in them you think you have eternal life; and these are they which testify of me" (John 5:39). Bishop B. F. Westcott points out that this word *search* is in the imperative mood; that is to say, our Lord was insisting that to find the Savior men must *search* the Scriptures. In their blindness, however, the scribes and Pharisees hopelessly failed to make this discovery, even though they were engaged in the most intense investigation of the Scriptures. They did not realize that searching, like reading, must be under the control of the Holy Spirit, if Christ is to be revealed. The Bible says, ". . . Eye has not seen, nor ear heard, nor have entered into the heart of man the things which God has prepared for those who love him. But God has revealed them to us through his Spirit. For the Spirit searches all things, yes, the deep things of God. . . . no one knows the things of God except the Spirit of God" (1 Cor. 2:9–11; see also vv. 12–14). So to know the truth there must be the obedience of our minds to the Word of God in *reading* and *searching* the truth until Christ is revealed by the Holy Spirit.

Illustration

In these days of selected readings and favorite passages, wrested texts, and promise boxes, here is helpful counsel. It was given by Dr. T. T. Shields to his students when he concluded a series of lectures on the Pentateuch. He told them: "I urge you to read consecutively through the entire Bible. Open your hearts to the martial strength of Joshua; the individual heroism of Judges; the sylvan beauty and domestic loveliness of Ruth; the philosophy of history, the sequence of cause and effect in the historical portions of the Old Testament; the philosophy of tears in the poetry of Job; the universality of the experimental utterances of David; the practical wisdom of Proverbs; the Preacher's appraisal of the vanity of things under the sun; the holy passion of the Canticles; the seraphic fire of Isaiah; the threnodies of Jeremiah; the supernal splendor of Ezekiel's visions of God; the foresight of Daniel; the pathos of Hosea; the periscopic and telescopic discernment of all the minor prophets, until you open the New Testament and read, 'When Jesus was born in Bethlehem of Judea in the days of Herod the King.' [Here] you will breathe the atmosphere of Genesis, and find principles reminiscent of Exodus, and feel as well as reason that the same Author speaks in every book. Read the Gospels, read the story of the crucifixion and of the resurrection, and gather with the apostles as the Holy Spirit descends. Read through the Acts. One by one the witnesses slip away, while their history recurs in part in the Epistles. Then read John's vision on the Isle of Patmos, and on through the book of Revelation, and you will hear the same Voice which has been speaking through all the Temple of Truth, saying, 'Surely I come quickly,' and you will be able to respond, 'Even so, come, Lord Jesus.' When you have finished it all, I know you will say, 'It is God's book. Nobody but God could speak like that.'"[2]

B. There Must Be Obedience of Heart

The apostle reminds his readers at Rome that they were once slaves to sin, but now they ". . . *obeyed from the heart* that form of doctrine to which [they] were delivered" (Rom. 6:17–18). To obey with the heart means more than just believing the truth. So many of us *assent* to truth but we do not *consent* to it! Just as a sinner can never be born into the kingdom of God without receiving what he believes, so no saint can progress in the life of discipleship without receiving what he believes. James says: "Therefore lay aside all filthiness and overflow of wickedness, and *receive* with meekness the implanted word, which is able to save your souls" (James 1:21). We must not fool with God. If we mean business then with docility and humility we must obey the truth of God from the heart.

Amplification

One of J. W. Chapman's rules for Bible study was this: "Live the truth you get in the morning through each hour of the day." Ultimately, it is not a matter of how often we go through the Bible, but how often the Bible goes through us. Some books are produced for our information. The Bible was produced for our transformation. There is nothing in the Bible that benefits you unless it is transmuted into life, unless it becomes a part of yourself, just like food. Unless you assimilate it and it becomes body, bone and muscle, it does you no good.[3]

C. There Must Be Obedience of Will

A phrase in Philippians 2:8 sums up the obedience of will: It is ". . . obedient to the point of death. . . ."

Before this could happen in the life of God's Servant he had to pray, ". . . Father, . . . not My will, but Yours, be done" (Luke 22:42). The cross represents the fulfillment of God's redemptive purpose for every life. Therefore, obedience is never valid until it becomes obedience unto death. This involves willingness to obey God—cost what it will—until the divine will is accomplished.

Illustration

Two friends were out walking in the mountains. Following hard at the heels of his master was a faithful dog. The dog's ears and eyes were listening and watching for words of command from his master. In conversation, the master began gesturing. He raised his arm in the direction of a precipice. The faithful dog, thinking that his master was giving a word of command to him, instantly leaped to his death over the precipice. Oh, that we were as quick to obey our master's commands, to have our ears "tuned to hear his slightest whisper," and then to obey from the heart—even unto death!

III. Experience of the Word of Truth

". . . the truth shall make you free" (John 8:32). If there is faithful continuance in the truth and soulful obedience to the truth, there will be joyful experience of the truth. This experience is summed up in one word: freedom (8:32). These words were addressed to people who claimed political freedom but, in reality, they were the slaves of Rome. They claimed religious freedom, but instead were slaves to the letter of the law. They claimed moral freedom, but in point of fact were slaves to sin. Nevertheless, it was to slaves like these that Jesus said, ". . . the truth shall make you free" (8:32). The Savior was offering them—and men and women ever since:

A. Personal Freedom

". . . if the Son makes you free, you shall be free indeed" (8:36). The Jews had just remarked to Christ, ". . . We are Abraham's descendants, and have never been in bondage to anyone. How can you say, 'You will be made free'?" (8:33). People have been saying this since the dawn of time to cover up their bondage to people. All of us are dominated by what others think and say. H. G. Wells once stated that the voice of our neighbors sounds louder in our ears than the voice of God; and it was Solomon who stated that ". . . the fear of man brings a snare . . ." (Prov. 29:25). Jesus can set you free from such bondage through the Word of God and the Spirit of God. The reason we are not the radiant and fearless witnesses we ought to be is because of our bondage to men.

One of the Reformers was told, "All the world is against you," to which he replied, "Then I am against the world." The epitaph on the tomb of John Knox reads: "Here lies the man who never feared the face of clay."

B. Literal Freedom

". . . the truth shall make you free" (8:32). The divine law without the divine life is bondage; the Word of God without the Spirit of God is slavery; but when the truth is obeyed in mind, heart, and will it sets men free. The law of God becomes a way of life, the Word of God becomes a path of life, the gospel of God becomes the aim of life. Literal freedom is the liberty to speak, preach, and write with confidence and conviction. Once a person has been set free in this area there is no influence for good that he cannot exert.

C. Spiritual Freedom

". . . the Spirit of life in Christ Jesus has made me free from the law of sin and death" (Rom. 8:2). Jesus had just told his listeners that "... whoever commits sin is a slave of sin" (John 8:34). How true this is! Discipleship breaks the chains that bind us to our sins and enables us to be the persons we know we ought to be. Discipleship implies freedom through the Son of God, by the Word of God, and in the power of the Spirit of God.

Illustration

Herod could incarcerate John the Baptist and finally behead him, but John was free while his captor was a slave although he was called king; Nero was the slave while Paul was God's free man, shouting, "I can do all things through Christ who strengthens me," in a Roman prison. King James could imprison that humble tinker, John Bunyan, for preaching on the streets of Bedford but Bunyan was free in a soul that reveled in spiritual visions and delights. Madame Guyon was imprisoned in the lonely Bastille prison but she was free in heart.

Do you know this spiritual freedom, or are you under the dominion of sin, compelled to give way to evil tempers and lusts—a servant of the experience of Romans 7? If so, move over into the eighth chapter and shout, "... the law of the Spirit of life in Christ Jesus has made me free from the law of sin and death."[4]

Conclusion

Here, then, is the threefold responsibility of true discipleship: continuance in the truth, obedience to the truth, and experience of the truth, as revealed by the Spirit of God and released by the Son of God. Christ says to us again: "... If you abide in my word, you are my disciples indeed. And you shall know the truth, and the truth shall make you free" (John 8:31–32). God make us disciples indeed!

3

The Disciple's Requirements

Luke 14:25–35; 9:57–62

"Whosoever doth not bear his cross, and come after me, cannot be my disciple . . . likewise, whosoever he be of you that foresaketh not all that he hath, he cannot be my disciple" (14:27, 33, KJV).

Introduction

The School of Discipline has its responsibilities, but it has also its requirements—which are vigorous and demanding. It is willingness to meet those requirements that distinguishes the nominal believer from the committed disciple. So we find that Jesus addressed the requirements of discipleship to the individual within the crowd. While great multitudes were following him, the master's call was to "any man" (14:26). What a challenge there is in these requirements of discipleship! In the first place, discipleship requires:

I. No Rival in the Life for Christ

"If any man come to me, and hate not . . ." (14:26).
Christian discipleship means giving one's first loyalty to
the Lord Jesus Christ; anything less than this is virtual
treason, if Jesus is truly Lord. There is no other response
than that of full submission to his sovereignty. This is the
only explanation to the master's use of the word "hate."
Since there is no place in Jesus' teaching for literal hatred,
he must have intended to convey the quality of love which
he expected of his followers. Anything less than this
would be hatred by comparison.

There is a deeper meaning here. I believe that Jesus is
making a clear distinction between redemptive love, which
is divine, and possessive love, which is human. If our relationship to our loved ones does not flow out of redemptive love it will not last. This is why possessive love is
basically selfish, and therefore doomed to failure. When
Jesus Christ is unrivaled in our lives then we love him
first, and the overflow of that love reaches out to family,
friends, and even foes. In practical terms, this means:

A. We may have a father and enjoy his loving attention but he cannot rival the Lord Jesus.
B. We may have a mother and enjoy her loving affection but she cannot rival the Lord Jesus.
C. We may have a wife and enjoy her loving devotion
   but she cannot rival the Lord Jesus.
D. We may have children and enjoy their loving submission but they cannot rival the Lord Jesus.
E. We may have brothers and sisters and enjoy their
   loving friendship and fellowship but they cannot
   rival the Lord Jesus.
F. We may have self-life and enjoy its loving ambition but it cannot rival the Lord Jesus.

Illustration

When V. Raymond Edman was a missionary in Ecuador he knew an earnest and effective layman who felt called to the ministry; but his wife would not hear of it. She threatened all manner of reprisal if he should leave his lucrative employment to become a servant of Jesus Christ. One evening he came to Brother Edman with a bundle under one arm, and tears in his eyes. The good doctor read to him from Mark 10:29–30: "Verily I say unto you, There is no man that hath left house, or brethren, or sisters, or father, or mother, or wife, or children, or lands, for my sake, and the gospel's, but he shall receive an hundredfold now in this time, houses, and brethren, and sisters, and mothers, and children, and lands, with persecutions; and in the world to come eternal life." After prayer and tears, Edman inquired what the man had in the bundle. "It contains my working clothes," he replied. "I left my employment today." He had counted the cost, and had set himself to leave all, and to face whatever persecutions might come; only that he might be Jesus' disciple. Do we wonder that he won his wife to full allegiance to the Master, and that together they have become pillars in the house of God?[1]

God has declared that ". . . in all things [Christ must] have the preeminence" (Col. 1:18). Can I, therefore, give him any less? A thousand times NO! For in doing so I would reveal that I have a rival in my life, and am a traitor to Christ. Discipleship demands that Christ should reign unrivaled in my heart, having preeminence in my thinking, speaking, and acting. If you, my friend, have a rival in your heart, God help you to pray:

> Jesus, thy boundless love to me
> No thought can reach, no tongue declare;
> Then [bend] my wayward heart to Thee,
> And reign without a rival there.
>
> Paul Gerhardt

II. No Refusal in the Life for Christ

". . . whosoever doth not bear his cross, and come after me, cannot be my disciple" (14:27). The disciples, no doubt, had seen a man take up his cross, and they knew what it meant. It was a one-way journey; he would never come back. Taking up the cross means the utmost in self-denial. Dietrich Bonhoeffer reminds us that when Jesus Christ calls us to follow him he calls us to die.[2] In the final analysis, bearing the cross means kneeling in Gethsemane and saying an eternal yes to all the will of God.

> This is the path the Master trod,
> Should not the servant tread it still?

To understand the deeper significance of saying yes to the implications of the cross, we need to study what Paul has to say about the cross in our daily lives, as set out in his epistle to the Galatians. Three important verses should be noted:

A. Bearing the Cross Means No Refusal to Die to the Principle of the Old Life

"I am crucified with Christ . . ." (Gal. 2:20). The old principle was "Not Christ, but I"; the new principle is "Not I, but Christ"; that is, a life with the "I" crossed out, and God's will supreme in everything.

In Gethsemane, the Lord Jesus could say, ". . . not my will, but thine, be done" (Luke 22:24). He could say throughout his lifetime, ". . . Lo, I come: in the volume of the book it is written of me, I delight to do thy will, O my God: yea, thy law is within my heart" (Ps. 40:7–8). Once we have learned this application of the cross to our self-life we have solved the problem of making the right decisions in our lives. We no longer ask, "Should I do this, or go there, or marry so-and-so?" The issue is not what we want to do, but rather what Christ wants to do in us and through us.

B. Bearing the Cross Means No Refusal to Die to the Passions of the Old Life

". . . they that are Christ's have crucified the flesh with the affections and lusts" (Gal. 5:24). Instead of responding to the calls of the old nature, we set our affections on things above; that is, we transmute, or sublimate, those very passions, desires, and hungers that have gone through death and the grave, to the higher purpose of the RISEN life. This means that Christ reigns in our passion life, and we ". . . make [no] provisions for the flesh, to fulfill the lusts thereof" (Rom. 13:14).

Illustration

My Soul Is All I Have

I am resolved I will not be
The dupe of things I touch and see;
These figured totals lie to me—
My soul is all I have.

Illusive cheats are goods and gold:
These chattels that I have and hold
Are preys of moth, and rust, and mold;
My soul is all I have.

A builder, I, but not with stone;
The self I am, nor flesh nor bone:
My house will 'dure when stars are gone;
My soul is all I have.

For me to traffic with my soul
Would make me brother to the mole;
The whole world's wealth were but a dole;
My soul is all I have.

I must take care I do not lean
T'ward what is sordid, false, or mean;

I must not touch the thing unclean;
My soul is all I have.

Oh, Keeper of the souls of men,
Keep mine for me from hurt or stain,
For, should it slip my hand—what then?
My soul is all I have!

                                        T. O. Chisholm

C. Bearing the Cross Means No Refusal to Die to the Program of the Old Life

". . . God forbid that I should glory, save in the cross of our Lord Jesus Christ, by whom the world is crucified unto me, and I unto the world" (Gal. 6:14). The old program was "Go *with* the world"; the new program is "Go *into* the world"; no longer pandering to the world, but preaching to the world and entering into the risen Christ's thought for the world when he said, ". . . Go ye into all the world, and preach the gospel to every creature" (Mark 16:15).

Bearing the cross, therefore, means no refusal to die to the principle, passions, and program of the old life. Christ is supreme in my life: controlling the *principle-room* of my will, the *passion-room* of my heart, and the *program-room* of my mind. This is the secret of dynamic discipleship.

III. No Retreat in the Life for Christ

". . . whosoever he be of you that forsaketh not all that he hath, he cannot be my disciple" (14:33). Forsaking all is following the Lord Jesus without retreat. This is vividly illustrated in Luke 9, verses 57–62. Three vignettes are recorded there of would-be followers of the Lord Jesus. In each case he made clear that forsaking all meant no retreat. In specific terms, this means:

A. No Tiring in the Life of Discipleship

". . . It came to pass, that, as they went in the way, a certain man said unto him, Lord, I will follow thee whithersoever thou goest. And Jesus said unto him, Foxes have holes, and birds of the air have nests; but the Son of man hath not where to lay his head" (9:57–58). There was nothing wrong with the way this young man offered his allegiance. His only problem was that he did not reckon with the cost of discipleship. Animals and birds have their places of habitation, but the Son of man has nowhere to lay his head (9:58). What a glimpse this is into the life of our Lord and the cost of the incarnation! It also teaches us that while here on earth we are not promised luxurious living, or beds of ease. It is so easy to respond with enthusiasm at the outset, but are we prepared to follow him to the end?

B. No Trifling in the Life of Discipleship

"And [Jesus] said unto another, Follow me. But he said, Lord, suffer me first to go and bury my father. Jesus said unto him, Let the dead bury their dead: but go thou and preach the kingdom of God" (9:59–60). With a little understanding of the background it becomes evident that this young man's father had not just died. The Jews counted a burial ritual as most important. The duty of burial took precedence over the study of the Law, the temple service, the observance of circumcision, and the reading of the Megillah.[3] What the young man was actually implying was a little more subtle. In effect, he was suggesting that he would gladly follow the Lord Jesus once his father was dead and he had entered into his inheritance. This would ensure that he had financial security to fall back on, should Christ's cause not succeed. The master's response was sharp and searching: ". . . Let the dead bury their dead: but go thou and preach the kingdom of God" (9:60). The young man was talking the language of the unregenerate, which was in direct contrast to the demands of the kingdom. Jesus could not wait for all the conveniences of the young man's self-interest.

Illustration

John MacNeil, the Scottish evangelist, was once talking about the excuses people make for not completely following Christ. Referring to the man who wished to first go and bury his father, he exclaimed with disgust, "Why, this poor fellow wanted a gravedigger's shovel, when our Lord was trying to give him a resurrection trumpet!" God's choices for us may be difficult, but we may be sure that they are the best. Are we willing to "leave all" and go on to the "more abundant life" of discipleship?[4]

C. No Turning in the Life of Discipleship

"And another also said, Lord, I will follow thee: but let me first go bid them farewell, which are at home at my house. And Jesus said unto him, No man, having put his hand to the plough, and looking back, is fit for the kingdom of God" (9:61–62). This third man, like the first, offered his services, but he interposed a condition that he must say farewell to those at home. At first this seems reasonable enough; but in this case it evidently concealed some reluctance on his part to take the decisive step. So Jesus points out that the kingdom of God has no room for those who look back when they are called forward.

Illustration

Often when converts from Hinduism inform their parents of their intention to be baptized it is not long before mother and father travel to the mission house and plead, with tears and threats, that they not take a step so fatal. Failing by this means to shake their children's resolutions, they become resigned to the fact. Their only stipulation is that the convert pay them one parting visit—to "bid them farewell which are at home at [his] house." The request seems reasonable. After all, to refuse is to wound parental feeling. So though his heart is with his spiritual brothers and he announces his soon return, the convert goes—*but never returns.* How often a farewell at home proves to be a farewell to Christ![5]

The cause of failure in true Christian discipleship can be traced to this problem of turning back. For example, Lot's wife retreated and became a monument to uselessness and shame (see Gen. 19:26). On the other hand, Jephthah would not go back and became a monument of usefulness and sacrifice (see Judges 11:35).

Conclusion

The issue of this message, then, is our willingness to meet these requirements of discipleship. They are going to cost; but before you say "too costly," view them in the light of Calvary love, and then with soberness and sincerity say:

> Dear Lord, in full surrender at Thy feet,
> I make my consecration vows complete:
> My life I yield to Thee;
> Henceforward, there shall be
> No rival, no refusal, no retreat.
>   Stephen F. Olford

4

The Disciple's Recognition
John 13:33–35

"Love one another. . . . By this all will know that you are My disciples . . ." (13:34–35).

Introduction

Every truth in the Word of God has its importance, so that it is impossible to pit one against the other. An aspect of teaching which calls for urgent expression in daily life is this matter of the disciple's recognition. When the Savior urged his disciples to "love one another" it was to be the hallmark by which his followers were to be recognized throughout all time. The threefold sense in which this mark is to be recognized may be formulated as follows:

I. Disciples Must Always Be Known by Redemptive Love

". . . love one another," commanded the Savior, "as I have loved you . . ." (13:34). When the Lord Jesus uttered these words he had just exemplified redemptive love by humbling himself to wash the feet of Judas, who was to betray him: of Peter, who was to deny him: and of the rest, who were to forsake him. But notwithstanding their failures and faults, he loved them all "to the end" (13:1). Such love is more than human love, it is essentially divine, and is only made available through the redemption that is in Christ Jesus.

John, in his first epistle, contrasts the difference between the absence of redemptive love and the presence of redemptive love:

A. The Absence of Redemptive Love

"In this the children of God and the children of the devil are manifest: Whoever does not practice righteousness is not of God, nor is he who does not love his brother" (1 John 3:10). Note again: ". . . He who does not love his brother abides in death. Whoever hates his brother is a murderer . . ." (1 John 3:14–15). By the word "hate" John is thinking of Cain, who is the prototype of jealousy and inward hatred which an unregenerate man can feel against his brother. "If someone says, 'I love God,' and hates his brother, he is a liar . . ." (1 John 4:20). Absence of redemptive love can lead to unrighteousness and hatred, in relation to others.

Illustration

There is a tradition that 300 priests with their trumpets and 300 rabbis with their scholars once gathered in the Temple court to curse the Samaritans with all the curses in the Law of Moses. Nor were the Samaritans less eager in hating and annoying. At the Passover it was the Jews' custom to light bonfires on the Mount of Olives, a signal for other fires, till the Euphrates was reached, to send the message to exiled Jews. The Samaritans lighted rival bonfires on other days to confuse the watchers.[1]

B. The Presence of Redemptive Love

John continues, "We know that we have passed from death to life, because we love the brethren . . ." (1 John 3:14); and again: "He who loves his brother abides in the light. . . . let us love one another, for love is of God; and everyone who loves is born of God . . ." (1 John 4:7). Redemptive love is the result of being born of God, receiving eternal life, and abiding in the light. Human love may superficially impress men with its words and wag of the tongue, but it is only Calvary love that can express itself in action and in reality.

Illustration

Reuel Howe illustrates love in the story of a mother and her eight-year-old daughter. The girl did something which caused her to feel alienated from her mother. Although her mother tried her best to help, the daughter finally ran out of the room in anger and went upstairs. Seeing her mother's new dress laid out for a party that evening, she found scissors and vented her hostility by making incisions, thereby seeking to injure her mother. Later the mother came upstairs, saw the ruined dress, and wept. Soon the small daughter came into the room and whispered, "Mother." But there was no reply. "Mother, Mother," she repeated. Still no reply. "Mother, Mother, please," she continued. The mother responded, "Please what?" "Please take me back, please take me back," pleaded the girl. That is what love does; it takes people back. "Love never ends." It reaches out until redemption is realized.

II. Disciples Must Always Be Known by Reciprocal Love

". . . love . . . one another" (13:34). The world that knows only human love may talk about a person who is "unsociable," or speak of "that mean woman," but this attitude must never characterize a follower of our Lord. You may feel there are certain Christians you could never love, or you may avoid those who belong to a different denomination. Such thinking is unknown in the circle of true discipleship, for reciprocal love means:

A. Love Shared in Christ

Paul describes such sharing when he expresses his deep desire for the Colossians that their hearts might be ". . . knit together in love . . ." (Col. 2:2). The word *knit* conveys two ideas, in the original: the first is that of "bringing together"; the second, of "carrying along," as an audience would be carried along by a convincing argument. When the Lord Jesus becomes the center of our shared love we are brought together and carried along by a love which knows no differences, no distinctions, and no disharmonies.

Illustration

In her book, *Living with Love,* Josephine Robertson tells of a youthful clergyman, the Rev. Joe Roberts, who arrived by stagecoach in a blizzard to minister to the Indians of Wyoming. Soon after his arrival the son of the chief was shot by a soldier in a brawl, and the chief vowed to kill the first white man he met. Thinking this could lead to a long, bloody feud, Roberts decided to take action. Seeking out the tepee, fifteen miles away in the mountains, Roberts stood outside and called the chief's name. When the chief appeared, Roberts said, "I know that the other white men have families, but I am alone. Kill me instead." Amazed, the chief motioned him inside his tent, where he asked, "How do you have so much courage?" Joe Roberts told him about Christ: His death, His teachings. When Joe left, the chief of the Shoshones had renounced his vow to kill and resolved to be a Christian. He had seen love in action. Every group which calls itself Christian should decide what it can do to make love visible in the home, the church, and the world. For unless love becomes visible it is not love at all.

B. Love Shown in Christ

". . . love one another" (13:34). Such love is the unstinted giving of ourselves for the good of others—spiritually, ethically, and practically.

Spiritually, Christ ". . . laid down His life for us. And we ought to lay down our lives for the brethren" (1 John 3:16). Think of the occasion when the crowds so thronged him that he and his disciples had no time to eat (see Mark 3:20); but he continued to give himself in preaching, teaching, and healing. Or recall the story in John 4 of the weary Savior who went miles out of his way in order to talk to one sin-sick soul (see John 4:4).

Paul, like his Lord, knew what it meant to lay down his life for the brethren. He could say, ". . . I will very gladly spend and be spent for your souls; though the more abundantly I love you, the less I am loved" (2 Cor. 12:15). Epaphroditus put the welfare of others before his own. Paul says of him, ". . . for the work of Christ he came close to death, not regarding his life . . ." (Phil. 2:30).

Illustration

When Wycliffe translator, Doug Meland and his wife moved into a village of Brazil's Fulnio Indians, he was referred to as "the white man," an uncomplimentary term, since other white men had exploited them, burned their homes, and robbed them of their lands. But after the missionaries learned the language and began to help the people with medicine and in other ways, they began to call Doug "the respectable white man." When the Melands began adopting the customs of the people, the Fulnio spoke of Doug as "the white Indian." Then one day, as Doug was washing the dirty, bloodcaked foot of an injured boy, he overheard a bystander say, "Who ever heard of a white man washing an Indian's foot before? Certainly this man is from God!" From that day on, whenever Doug entered an Indian home, it would be announced, "Here comes the man God sent us."[2]

Reciprocal love is then shown *ethically*. It is John who says, "He who loves his brother abides in the light, and there is no cause for stumbling [or scandal] in him" (1 John 2:10). This means that the true disciple *thinks love*. The central note in Paul's "Song of Love" is the clause, ". . . [Love] thinks no evil" (1 Cor. 13:5). Rather, he *speaks love*. A world of mischief and madness can be created by the uncontrolled tongue. James tells us that the tongue can set on fire the whole course of nature (see James 3:6). But the Christian who lives in the power of the ungrieved Spirit can bear ". . . with one another in love," speak ". . . the truth in love . . . ," and edify the body "in love" (Eph. 4:2, 15–16).

Illustration

A newspaper in Wales once carried this headline: "Poison Pen Sends a Woman to Death." The article went on to say that the lady committed suicide after receiving poisonous and anonymous letters and postcards for nine months.

The true disciple supremely *acts love*. Peter says, ". . . above all things have fervent love for one another, for 'love will cover a multitude of sins'" (1 Peter 4:8). To "cover a multitude of sins" does not imply compromise or weakness, for we are told to ". . . rebuke [sin] in the presence of all, that the rest also may fear" (1 Tim. 5:20). The idea behind Peter's words is rather that of the "elastic" love which stretches over the shortcomings of our brethren. This is the love that is more ready to forgive than to expose and judge.

Reciprocal love is also shown *practically*. John asks the question, ". . . whoever has this world's goods, and sees his brother in need, and shuts up his heart from him, how does the love of God abide in him?" (1 John 3:17). This was no theoretical idealism in the early church. Think of the beginning of the church. We read that ". . . all who believed were together, and had all things in common, and sold their possessions and goods, and divided them among all, as anyone had need" (Acts 2:44–45). Then consider the church as established at Jerusalem. We read: ". . . And great grace was upon them all. Nor was there anyone among them who lacked . . . and they distributed to each as anyone had need" (Acts 4:33–35). Once more, reflect on the churches throughout Macedonia. We read "that in a great trial of affliction the abundance of their joy and their deep poverty abounded in the riches of their liberality" (2 Cor. 8:2).

What was true of the churches was also true of individuals. Think of Barnabas who, "having land, sold it, and brought the money and laid it at the apostles' feet" (Acts 4:37).

From these illustrations of reciprocal and practical giving we must not deduce a wrong conception of our responsibility in stewardship. God does not call us to sell up and distribute our goods without demand or discrimination. He does, however, challenge our love in relation to its *willingness.* If and when the occasion demands, we must be ever ready to give that willingness practical expression.

John Wesley's rule for Christian living was just this: "Do all the good you can, by all the means you can, in all the ways you can, in all the places you can, at all the times you can, to all the people you can, as long as ever you can."[3]

III. Disciples Must Always Be Known by Reflected Love

"By this all will know that you are My disciples . . . ," said Jesus (13:35). Followers of great teachers have their distinctive marks. The world outside recognizes a given teacher by that which is reflected in his students. This was true of the disciples of Jesus. They had to reflect redemptive and reciprocal love in a manner which would convince the world that they were his disciples. This was to be expressed outwardly in two ways; first, through:

A. The Reflected ONENESS of Love

Jesus prayed that this oneness might be fulfilled in his disciples so that the world would believe that he had been sent by the Father and that they were also loved by him (see John 17:21–23). The apologists of the first centuries delighted in appealing to the striking fact of the common love of Christians, which was a new thing in the history of mankind; and while the Church has sometimes forgotten the characteristic, the world never has. Tertullian records in a famous passage how "the heathen were wont to exclaim with wonder, 'See how these Christians love one another!'"

Illustration

Dolly Madison, wife of the fourth president of the United States, was one of the most popular women in American history. Wherever she went she charmed and captivated everyone. Asked to explain the secret of her power over others, she exclaimed, "I have none, I desire none. I merely love everyone." Those who love are richly rewarded by love returned.

B. The Reflected WITNESS of Love

John reminds us: ". . . If we love one another, God abides in us, and His love has been perfected in us. . . . And we have seen and testify that the Father has sent the Son as Savior of the world" (1 John 4:12, 14). Nothing is so universal in its appeal, so powerful in its impact, and so wonderful in its effect, as the *witness* of love. The world is starved for love and waits eagerly for church members to reflect the love of Christ. The tragedy is that there is so little reflected oneness, and therefore no convincing witness. Even Chrysostom, in his day, lamented that division among Christians was hindering the conversion of the heathen. How easy it is to lose our first love. May God rekindle his love in all our hearts! The witness of love is not only a ministry to the church, it is a service to the world. Men and women will never believe our message until they see and sense our genuine love for them.

Illustration

A Christian woman working among the prostitutes of London found a young girl desperately ill in a cold and bare room. She ministered to her by changing her bed linen, supplying food and medicine, and making the place warm and cheerful. When she thought she had gained the confidence of the girl, the worker offered to say a prayer, but was rebutted with the words, "No, you don't care for me; you're doing this just to get to heaven." Weeks went by in which God's servant worked tirelessly to restore the girl to full health. One day the woman worker said, "My dear, you are nearly well now, and I must leave you to tend the needs of others. Before I go, I want to kiss you goodbye." The pure lips that had known only prayer and holy words met the lips defiled by oaths and lustful caresses. In that moment the girl's heart broke. Love conquered and another soul was won for the kingdom.

Conclusion

God's way is love's way. May we be characterized by the redemptive, reciprocal, and reflected love of Christ, and so be known always as the disciples of Jesus.

The Disciple's Realization
John 15:7–16

"By this my Father is glorified, that you bear much fruit; so you will be my disciples" (15:8).

Introduction

When Jesus said these words he was revealing the disciple's great realization. If fruitfulness glorified God, then nothing less than abundant fruitfulness should constitute the realization of every true disciple. Most commentators agree that the clause, "By this my Father is glorified," coordinates three aspects of fruitfulness, in verses 7, 8, and 16, or what we shall call:

I. Fruitfulness in the Prayer Life

"If you abide in me, and my words abide in you, you will ask what you desire, and it shall be done for you"

(15:7). This statement of the Savior makes it clear that fruitfulness in the prayer life must be commensurate with:

A. The Harmony of Requests in Prayer

"If you abide in me, and my words abide in you, you will ask . . ." (15:7). This means that if our wills are to be harmonized with God's will in requests that we make, we shall have to abide in Christ and allow his words to abide in us. Fruit ripens for picking as it abides in the sun and takes into its nature the cleansing and enriching rays. The same applies to our requests in prayer. They ripen for picking while we abide in Christ and in the process we take into our beings the cleansing and enriching properties of his word.

B. The Constancy of Replies to Prayer

". . . you will ask what you desire, and it shall be done for you" (15:7). Constant replies to prayer are the fruit of God's will brought to birth in our lives. This is why God is glorified in a fruitful prayer life. Jesus made this plain when he said, "And whatever you ask in my name, that I will do, that the Father may be glorified in the Son" (John 14:13). Remember that God is our Father and, therefore, longs to answer prayer. The measure in which he is glorified is the measure in which he can righteously answer bigger and bigger requests from us.

Illustration

No sublimer story has been recorded in earthy annals than that of David Brainerd. No miracle attests, with diviner force, the truth of Christianity than the life and work of this godly man. Alone in the savage wilds of America, struggling day and night with a mortal disease, unschooled in the care of souls, having access to the Indians for a large portion of time only through the bungling medium of a

pagan interpreter, with the Word of God in his heart and
in his hand, his soul fixed with the divine flame, a place
and time to pour out his heart and soul to God in prayer, he
fully established the worship of God and secured great
results. After spending a whole week in prayer he spoke
with such power that countless numbers of Indians were
led to yield their lives to God. The Indians were changed
from the lowest besotments of heathenism to pure, devout,
intelligent Christians.

Brainerd lived a life of holiness and prayer: by day and by
night he prayed. Before preaching and after preaching he
prayed. Riding through the interminable solitude of the for-
est he prayed. On his bed of straw he prayed. Morning,
noon, and night he communed with God. Little wonder he
had such power—God was with him mightily because he
lived in the presence of God.[1]

Is your prayer life a fruitful one? Are you conscious of
bringing to birth, in everyday life, God's will by the
requests you offer and the answers you receive? If not,
then you are not abiding in Christ, and discipleship, in all
its fullness, is not being realized in your life.

To glorify God, in the second instance, means that the
disciple must realize:

II. Fruitfulness in the Personal Life

"By this my Father is glorified, that you bear much
fruit . . ." (15:8). The fruit we are expected to produce in
personal life is spirituality. The apostle Paul describes this
fruit as one cluster: ". . . the fruit of the Spirit is love, joy,
peace, longsuffering, kindness, goodness, faithfulness, gentleness, self-control . . ." (Gal. 5:22–23). In this cluster we
have:

A. The Essence of Spirituality in Personal Life

". . . love, joy, peace . . ." (Gal. 5:22). Each of these three graces is fundamental to a personal experience of God in Christ. Love is the evidence of relationship to Christ, while joy and peace are the evidence of fellowship in Christ. Where relationship to Christ and fellowship in Christ do not exist there cannot be genuine spirituality. This may sound devastating, but it is true. Let me illustrate what I mean.

A man may be resplendent. He may possess all conceivable intellectual endowments, he may speak with the eloquence of angels, he may subdue the material world by conquering physical forces, and personally, he may embody the most charming combination of disposition and temperament—and yet not possess true spirituality. The reason for this is because natural endowments are distinct from the fruit of the Spirit. How important, then, that we should be sure of true essence of spirituality, namely, ". . . love, joy, peace . . ." (Gal. 5:22).

B. The Expression of Spirituality in Personal Life

". . . longsuffering, kindness, goodness . . ." (Gal. 5:22). While the essence of spirituality has to do with God, the expression of spirituality has to do with our fellow men. In the home, the church, and the world, we are to be known by our longsuffering, gentleness, and goodness. *Longsuffering* is that quality of patience, in the face of provocation, and the ability not to surrender or succumb under trial. *Kindness* is the spirit of serviceableness under all conditions; while *goodness* is the benevolence and generosity of the disciple at all times. Do others know us by our longsuffering, kindness, and goodness?

Illustration

Known as the "Bishop of the South Pacific," John Selwyn had at one time been recognized for his boxing skill. Touched by the Holy Spirit's convicting power, however, he later became an outstanding missionary. One day this saintly leader reluctantly gave a stern but loving rebuke to a man who regularly attended the local church. The disorderly one resented the advice and angrily struck Selwyn a violent blow in the face with his fist. In return the missionary folded his arms and humbly looked into the man's blazing eyes. With his boxing skill he could easily have knocked out his antagonist. Instead, he turned the other cheek and waited calmly to be hit a second time. This was too much for the assailant, who, greatly ashamed, fled into the jungle. Years later, the man accepted the Lord as his Savior and gave his testimony before the church. It was customary at that time for a believer to choose a Christian name for himself after conversion and he chose the name John Selwyn, adding, "He's the one who taught me what Jesus Christ is really like." Longsuffering had made the missionary's witness effective.

C. The Exercise of Spirituality in Personal Life

". . . faithfulness, gentleness, self-control . . ." (5:22–23). The exercise of spirituality has to do with the discipline of self, or the inward faithfulness, humbleness, and temperateness of life. To fail in this inward exercise is to spoil the balance and symmetry of the whole cluster of fruit.

Dr. J. Hamilton tells us that chemists have analyzed the fruit of the vine and found that there are nine ingredients that make up the grape juice we know so well. The extraordinary thing about this juice, however, is that it cannot be made up of one, or even two, berries. It can be produced only from the best specimens where the cluster is complete.

If God is to be glorified in the fruitfulness of our personal life, then the cluster of fruit must be complete. In other words, fruitfulness must be the essence, expression, and exercise of spirituality in us. Such fruitfulness will never be crude: it will always be finished; for it is not a process, but the result of many processes, the ultimate product of many forces working together.

Illustration

Imagine someone without experience sitting down before Raphael's famous picture of the transfiguration and attempting to reproduce it! How crude and lifeless his work would be! But if such a thing were possible that the spirit of Raphael should enter into the man and obtain mastery of his mind and eye and hand, it would be entirely possible that he could paint this masterpiece; for it would simply be Raphael reproducing Raphael. And this in a mystery is what is true of the disciple filled with the Holy Spirit. Christ by the Spirit dwells within him as a divine life, and Christ is able to image forth Christ from the interior life of the outward example.[2]

One more aspect of fruitfulness must engage our attention. For God to be glorified, the disciple must realize:

III. Fruitfulness in the Practical Life

"You did not choose me, but I chose you and appointed you that you should go and bear fruit, and that your fruit should remain . . ." (15:16). Observe that fruitfulness in practical life is:

A. Appointed Service

Said the Savior: ". . . I chose you and appointed you that you should go and bear fruit . . ." (15:16). We see that while personal fruitfulness relates to spirituality, practical fruitfulness has to do with service. Despite this distinction, however, it is important to recognize that practical fruitfulness is an extension of personal fruitfulness. Indeed, without personal fruitfulness practical fruitfulness would be impossible. Such fruitfulness is God's purpose of vocation for every Christian. So many people are confused and perplexed about life's vocation. They imagine that unless they are especially called to do what is termed "full-time Christian work," or to engage in some other spectacular employment, they are not fulfilling life's vocation. Nothing could be farther from the truth. Study the Savior's words in connection with other relevant Bible teaching and you will see that vocation is Christ working through his disciples in whatever sphere they are found. In this sense, every disciple is chosen, appointed, and sent to bear fruit to the glory of God. Bearing fruit is allowing the essence, expression, and exercise of the fruit of the Spirit in personal life to have its full impact within the context of our daily work and witness.

"But what about the mission field, or some other specific Christian vocation?" someone asks. The answer to that question is that direction to such fields of labor is the strategic placing of those who already are fulfilling a ministry. The responsibility of thrusting out laborers and distributing manpower is God's. Our business is to accept the work at hand as a vocation, in the spirit of discipleship, and "stay put" until he directs otherwise.

Illustration

Every Christian should think of himself as having a divine call. L. C. Hester of Whitehours, Texas is a plumber. Every time he goes out on a job he packs a New Testament in with his tools. Consequently, he has earned the title "the witnessing plumber." A minister said of him: "That witnessing plumber has won hundreds to Christ since he became a Christian. Many will listen to a working man who will not listen to a preacher."

B. Abiding Service

"... your fruit should remain ..." (15:16). If our fruit is to remain we must be very careful to distinguish between fruit and fungus! We must surely affirm with all honesty that much activity that goes on in the name of fruit is really nothing more than fungus, and fungus is a parasite which is not only foreign to God's work, but actually saps its very life.

Illustration

In Mexico and the tropical zones of South America a so-called "strangler" fig grows in abundance. The Spanish-speaking people refer to it as the *matapalo* which means "the tree killer." The fruit is not palatable except to cattle and the fowls of the air. After the birds eat it, they must clean their beaks of the sticky residue. They do this by rubbing them on nearby trees. The seeds of the small fig have a natural glue which makes them adhere to the branches. When the rainy season arrives, germination takes place. Soon tiny roots make their way down into the heart of the wood and begin to grow. Within a few years the once lovely palms have become entirely covered with the entangling vines of the parasitic growth. Unless the tree is set free through the removal of these "strangler" figs, it finally begins to wither, dropping one frond after another until it is completely lifeless. The only way to stop the killing process is for someone to take a sharp knife and cut away the invader.

The only fruit which remains is that which is produced within the orbit of God's will. John declares, "... he who does the will of God abides forever" (1 John 2:17). Without doubt, the reason why so many evidences of D. L. Moody's work for God remain with us today is because that text made a tremendous impression upon his life; in fact, it appeared on a plaque in his office, and also on his tombstone.

If we want to see our fruit in service abide the day of testing and reward let us see to it that we are consciously fulfilling our vocation in the will of God. Such fruitfulness in practical life will glorify God, not only in eternity, but now in time.

Conclusion

We have seen that the disciple's realization is the glory of God in a fruitful prayer life, a fruitful personal life, and a fruitful practical life. Jesus taught that such fruitfulness has degrees of abundance: namely, "fruit," "more fruit," and "much fruit" (15:2, 5, 8). What glorifies the Father is clearly the "much fruit"; that is, *much* fruit in the prayer life, *much* fruit in the personal life, and *much* fruit in the practical life. This "much fruit" is what completes discipleship, both in realization and manifestation. God make us all developed disciples for his glory! To achieve this realization we must know what it is to be consciously, constantly, and conspicuously filled with the Holy Spirit. Only as the Spirit fills will love, joy, peace, longsuffering, kindness, goodness, faithfulness, gentleness, and self-control be seen in our practical life. Only then will our Father in heaven be glorified.

Part 2

God's Blueprint
for Church Membership

Christian Certainty

Romans 8:12–17, 26–39

"The Spirit Himself bears witness with our spirit that we are children of God" (8:16).

Introduction

It is possible to be a Christian and yet not enjoy Christian certainty. One of the devil's main devices is to rob the Christian of the *joy* of salvation—because he knows he cannot rob him of the *fact* of salvation. God's purpose for us is that we should know not only the fact, but the *fullness* of salvation.

It was a great day when you committed your life to Christ, but again and again the devil brings doubts into your mind as to whether or not that experience was genuine. Here's how you can be sure that you are a child of God:

I. The Word of God

Christian certainty is the faith which accepts and rests on the Word of God. A study of the Bible reveals that:

A. The Word of God Presents Christian Certainty

". . . these [signs] are written that you may believe that Jesus is the Christ, the Son of God, and that believing you may have life in his name" (John 20:31); and again: "These things I have written to you who believe in the name of the Son of God, that you may *know* that you have eternal life, and that you may . . . believe in the name of the Son of God" (1 John 5:13). God has preserved this precious Book throughout the centuries so that we may have something upon which to rest our faith. God has spoken through this revelation, and he tells us that to believe on the name of his Son is to KNOW that we have eternal life.

D. L. Moody once remarked, "I believe hundreds of Christians have not got the assurance of salvation just because they are not willing to take God at his Word."

B. The Word of God Produces Christian Certainty

Three verses from the New Testament show this: "Of his own will he brought us forth by the word of truth, that we might be a kind of firstfruits of his creatures" (James 1:18); "having been born again, not of corruptible seed but incorruptible, through the Word of God which lives and abides forever" (1 Peter 1:23); "by which have been given to us exceeding great and precious promises, that through these you may be partakers of the divine nature, having escaped the corruption that is in the world through lust" (2 Peter 1:4). Look at the combined significance of these verses. The first says that God effects the miracle of the new birth through his Word. The second tells us that it is like seed which is carried into our hearts; faith lays hold of it and life begins. The third verse shows that as God's promises are applied to our lives we become ". . . partakers of the divine nature . . ." (2 Peter 1:4).

C. The Word of God Promotes Christian Certainty

". . . faith comes by hearing, and hearing by the word of God" (Rom. 10:17); ". . . whatever things were written before were written for our learning, that we through the patience and comfort of the Scriptures might have hope" (Rom. 15:4). The more we read, hear, and heed the Word of God, the stronger becomes our faith, love, hope, patience, and testimony.

So Christian certainty is based on the Word of God. It does not depend on feelings; that is merely a by-product. Feelings change, depending on our temperament, background, and circumstances. It is not a question of feeling, but a matter of fact.

Illustration

Three people were walking up a mountainside. The one in front was called Mr. Fact; the middle one, Mr. Faith; and the third, Mr. Feelings. When Mr. Faith looked at Mr. Feelings he stumbled and made no progress. Then someone called to him: "Keep your eyes on Mr. Fact, not Mr. Feelings!" He obeyed and made the grade and soon reached the summit.

Don't worry if the devil comes and whispers that this or that is not true. Remember that you never had doubt before—which is one of the evidences that you are converted. In that sense doubts are healthy; but they become dangerous when you allow them to conceive and bring forth unbelief.

Illustration

A little boy had been gloriously converted. Before going to bed that night he read the text the evangelist had given him: "He who has the Son has life; he who does not have the Son of God does not have life" (1 John 5:12). "I have life," he said, "for I have received the Son." A voice seemed to say from somewhere underneath the bed, "No, you haven't." "Yes, I have," he replied. "No, you haven't" the voice insisted. And so the argument went back and forth. Finally, Johnny got up, put on the light, and found the text. He read it aloud: "He who has the Son has life. . . ." Again he seemed to hear the voice saying, "No, you don't." Taking his open Bible, he pushed it under the bed and said, "There you are, read it for yourself!"

That is how the Lord Jesus met the devil in the wilderness. When the enemy came and tried to sow doubts in His mind, Jesus said, "It is written," "It is written," "It is written" (Matt. 4:4, 7, 10).

II. The Work of Christ

Christian certainty is the faith which accepts and rests upon the work of Christ—all that he did for us on Calvary's cross and in resurrection triumph. The work of Christ guarantees the certainty of:

A. The Believer's Justification

". . . being justified freely by his grace through the redemption that is in Christ Jesus" (Rom. 3:24); ". . . God demonstrates his own love toward us, in that while we were still sinners, Christ died for us. Much more then, having now been justified by his blood, we shall be saved from wrath through him" (Rom. 5:8–9). The word "justification" is a legal term and denotes "made right," or "made to appear before God in a favorable light." When addressing children, we sometimes say, "Justified means just as if I had never sinned."

The Bible reminds us that we are all sinners (see Rom. 3:23; 6:23) and stand condemned before the bar of God. We are not only sinners by nature, but sinners by practice. Then we hear the gospel—the Good News—that Jesus Christ, in love, came to pay the penalty for a broken law (see 1 Peter 2:24), and we believe and accept the pardon he has provided. Now we are justified, acquitted, made to appear before God in a favorable light, and God will never reverse that word of acquittal.

The act of justification positions the believer in Christ.

Illustration

A lady who possessed a valuable diamond ring was once walking along a street in Paris. In pulling off her glove she dislodged her ring, which rolled along the ground and dropped through a grating into a drain. Greatly distressed, she peered down into the catch basin, which was full of black, watery mud. She tried to retrieve her treasure with the end of her umbrella, but her efforts proved fruitless. In desperation, she finally rolled up her sleeve, plunged her arm deep into the black muck, and in a few minutes retrieved the ring. A Christian standing nearby was reminded of the Scripture in Psalm 40:2. He thought, "Has not Jesus done much more for me? I had nothing in me that was worthy; rather I was sinful, rebellious, and unlovely, but he was willing to come from heaven's glory, take me out of the horrible pit of sin, position me in Christ, and set me among the princes in glory. Yes, Jesus saves from the guttermost to the uttermost!"[1]

B. The Believer's Sanctification

"By that will we have been sanctified through the offering of the body of Jesus Christ once for all. . . . For by one offering he has perfected forever those who are being sanctified" (Heb. 10:10, 14). The verb *sanctified* means "to make holy," or "to set apart for God," "to reserve for God." Whereas there is a progressive sanctification in the believer's life, the thought before us is the *fact* of our sanctification. The moment a person receives Christ as Savior and Lord he is sanctified, in God's sight, and no devil in hell, no man on earth, or angel in heaven, can change that fact. God writes across our lives "Reserved"; we are his.

The act of sanctification preserves the believer in Christ.

C. The Believer's Glorification

". . . we know that all things work together for good to those who love God, to those who are the called according to his purpose. For whom he foreknew, he also predestined to be conformed to the image of his Son, that he might be the firstborn among many brethren. Moreover whom he predestined, these he also called; whom he called, these he also justified; and whom he justified, these he also glorified" (Rom. 8:28–30). However long it takes to accomplish it, God sees us as those who have been made just like his Son, and one day we shall live with him in heaven.

An African was once asked, "Do you think you will ever get to heaven?" With confidence and a smile from ear to ear, he replied, "I am as sure of heaven as if I were already there." And he was right, for if we are resting upon the work of Christ then God says we are justified, sanctified, and glorified.

The act of glorification perfects the believer in Christ.

The work of Christ is a finished work; nothing can be added to it. So many people think they will get to heaven by giving, praying, going to church, or doing other good works. But that is not what the Bible teaches. The Lord Jesus Christ has finished the work, and we are to rest upon that work. Although we are going to serve him in devotion and love, and give him our time, talents, and all that we have, it still is a fact—so far as our eternal destiny is concerned—that we cannot do anything to earn our salvation; it is a completed work.

Illustration

An evangelist was trying to lead a cabinetmaker to Christ. This man was brilliant in his work, yet he felt he had to do something to earn his salvation. One day the evangelist visited him in his shop and admired a piece of work the man had just finished. With mischief in his eyes, the evangelist picked up a plane and said, "I'm going to see if I can ease off this corner and put a finishing touch to it." At that the cabinetmaker was horrified, and cried, "Man alive! Don't do that, it's a finished article!" "That's what I've been trying to teach you for the last few weeks," said the evangelist. "The work of Christ for your salvation is a finished work. You can't add anything to it. All you have to do is accept it." The man saw the point and decided for Christ there and then.

III. The Witness of the Spirit

God the Father, God the Son, and God the Spirit are involved in the work of redemption. Christian certainty is the faith which accepts and rests on the witness of the Spirit. His indwelling presence gives us:

A. A New Sense of Relationship

". . . as many as are led by the Spirit of God, these are sons of God. For you did not receive the spirit of bondage again to fear, but you received the Spirit of adoption by whom we cry out 'Abba, Father.' The Spirit Himself bears witness with our spirit that we are the children of God" (Rom. 8:14–16). If I were to ask you if you knew what it meant to be a Christian you might nod your head in a nominal way. But if I were to probe deeper you might reply: "If that is what it means to be a Christian, then I don't know anything about it." But if the Spirit of God tells your inward spirit that you are a child of God, then you have the assurance that you are related to him.

B. A New Sense of Resourcefulness

". . . and if children, then heirs—heirs of God and joint heirs with Christ . . ." (Rom. 8:17). An heir is a person who is entitled to an inheritance. Think of the inheritance we have in our Lord Jesus Christ! Not only pardon, peace, joy, victory, a sense of purpose, and eternal life, but heaven as well! You have sensed your weakness; and turning to Christ he has given you strength. You have sensed your emptiness; and turning to Christ he has given you fullness. You have sensed your aimlessness; and turning to Christ he has given you direction. In short, you have proved, and will continue to prove, that there is no demand made upon your life, as a young Christian, which is not a demand on the life of Christ in you. All the resources of heaven are at your disposal. Corrie ten Boom once said, "Too many Christians live as beggars. It grieves the Father when we do not live as rich as he is."

C. A New Sense of Responsibility

". . . if indeed we suffer with him, that we may also be glorified together. For I consider that the sufferings of this present time are not worthy to be compared with the glory which shall be revealed in us" (Rom. 8:17–18). There may have been times when you laughed and jeered at Christians; but now you take your stand for Christ, even though it involves misunderstanding and unpopularity with your unregenerate friends. You do not mind suffering for the Lord; indeed, you count it a privilege to do so, like the early disciples who rejoiced ". . . that they were counted worthy to suffer shame for his name" (Acts 5:41). You have discovered that you *now* have a new sense of responsibility to live for Christ; you want to win others to him. That is because the Spirit of God has come into your life. This is the witness of the Spirit.

Remember the Word of God extends to us Christian certainty, the work of Christ ensures for us Christian certainty, the witness of the Spirit effects in us Christian certainty.

Conclusion

Praise God, we can rest with confidence upon this three-fold basis for the experience of Christian certainty. God grant us to sing and mean:

> Blessed assurance, Jesus is mine!
> Oh, what a foretaste of glory divine!
> Heir of salvation, purchase of God,
> Born of his Spirit, washed in his blood.
>   Fanny J. Crosby

7

Daily Devotions
Deuteronomy 8:1–14

"Man shall not live by bread alone; but man lives by every word that proceeds from the mouth of the LORD" (8:3).

Introduction

No one truly born of God would question that it is a commendable practice to have a daily quiet time with the Lord; in fact, it is absolutely vital to Christian growth and development. The Bible always associates the man of God with a strictly disciplined devotional life. Writing to his son in the faith, Timothy, Paul says: "All Scripture is given by inspiration of God, and is profitable for doctrine, for reproof, for correction, for instruction in righteousness, that the man of God may be complete, thoroughly equipped for every good work" (2 Tim. 3:16). When the Lord Jesus said, ". . . Man shall not live by bread alone, but by every word that proceeds from the mouth of God" (Matt. 4:4), he testified, once and for all, to the value of cultivating the devotional life. By "every word" he did not mean a casual reading of the Bible. The thought is rather "every spoken word," and it is only in the quiet place of communion and meditation that the man of God can hear (with the ears of his heart) the spoken Word. In order to help those who know nothing about a definite method in observing this necessary devotional habit, let me suggest some guidelines:

I. The Reasons for the Quiet Time

". . . Man shall not live by bread alone, but by *every word* that proceeds from the mouth of God" (Matt. 4:4). When the Lord Jesus spoke these words he testified, once and for all, to the value of the quiet time. What he was saying is that the whole Bible is for the whole man. Therefore, we cannot afford to miss any part of it, however difficult certain portions may be. Communion with God in the light of his Word is vital to:

A. Spiritual Constitution

". . . as newborn babes, desire the pure milk of the word, that you may grow thereby" (1 Peter 2:2); and for those further on in the Christian life, the writer to the Hebrews reminds us: ". . . solid food belongs to those who are of full age . . ." (Heb. 5:14). Peter is writing as a family man. He knew the experience of a father, or mother, waking up in the night to meet the cries of the young infant, the newly-born, who desires the milk by which he lives. God has built into every child at birth that insatiable desire for the very thing by which it lives. Peter implies that if there is no desire for "the pure milk of the word" then there is no new birth. It is impossible to subsist as a Christian without one's daily quiet time, because God has put into our spiritual life and nature a hunger for the Word.

For those who are more developed in the Christian life, it is even more important. So while there is milk for the very young there is meat for those who are full grown. It was because David realized the need for the spoken word for spiritual constitution and development that he prayed, ". . . Strengthen me according to Your word" (Ps. 119:28).

Illustration

S. L. Brengle, who worked with Gen. William Booth of the Salvation Army, once made this statement: "In eating, it is not the amount we eat, but the amount we digest that does us good; and just so it is in reading and studying. It is not the amount we read, but what we remember and make our own—that does us good."

B. Spiritual Correction

"All Scripture is given by inspiration of God, and is profitable for . . . correction" (2 Tim. 3:16). Nothing will cleanse and correct the life like the Word of God. In one of his psalms, David asks a question: "How can a young man cleanse his way? By taking heed according to your word" (Ps. 119:9). It was because the Lord recognized the correcting and cleansing power of the Word that he said to his disciples, after one of his discourses, "You are already clean because of the word which I have spoken to you" (John 15:3). The word is the means by which we are being daily cleansed (see John 17:17).

Illustration

The Bible is man's living manual. When you buy an automobile or a washing machine, you receive a manual of operation for the machinery. It tells you how to operate it, how to service it, how to make necessary adjustments, what to look for if trouble develops, and so forth. The Bible is like that. . . . To ignore the Word of God is to face certain disaster. . . . God is the Master Mechanic; he made us and he can keep us operating effectively; he gave us an operator's manual to aid us in life and living.[1]

C. Spiritual Counsel

"All Scripture . . . is profitable . . . for instruction in righteousness" (2 Tim. 3:16). "Give me understanding according to Your word," says David in Psalm 119:169. And in Psalm 73:24 the psalmist's constant assurance was, "You will guide me with Your counsel . . .". The Bible is not so much a book of rules as a book of principles. The more we read the Word of God, the more his principles of righteousness are inculcated. No man can be guided by the Spirit who isn't a Bible-mastered man. The reason Christians are tentative and unsure about areas of decision is because they are not people of the Word of God. All wisdom and knowledge are embodied in Jesus Christ and he is revealed in the pages of Scripture. "If any [man] lacks wisdom, let him ask of God, who gives to all liberally and without reproach, and it will be given to him" (James 1:5). God never gives wisdom that is contrary to the revealed Word. To know a guided life we must know what it is to read the Word *day by day.*

D. Spiritual Conflict

". . . the sword of the Spirit . . . is the Word of God," says Paul with victorious confidence (see Eph. 6:17). The context of this passage is spiritual warfare (see 6:11–12), and in the light of these tremendous odds we are to have our defensive armor on, which is Christ in his totality (Chrysostom). The offensive weapons that Paul mentions are prayer and the Word of God (6:17–18). Prayer sights the enemy while the word fights the enemy.

How did the Savior overcome the devil in the wilderness? It was the spoken Word of God every time. No doubt his quotations from Deuteronomy were the very passages on which he had been meditating with his God during those forty days and nights. Isaiah tells us that every day his ear was open to hear the voice of his Father; he was not rebellious (Isa. 50:4–5). Three times the devil attacked him, and those temptations constitute every temptation with which man is confronted. Satan attacked him along the lines of the body, the soul, and the spirit. Each time he replied, "It is written," "It is written," "It is written" (Matt. 4:4, 7, 10), and with those Spirit-thrusts he defeated the enemy. As God of very God, he could have pulverized the devil, once for all, but he didn't. He reserved the right to withhold the prerogatives of his deity and, as Man—depending on the Word of God and the Spirit of God—he beat the devil.

II. The Requirements for the Quiet Time

These are purely suggestive and practical. Needless to say, start with:

A. A Good Bible

with clear print, and one in which you can enter a few notes. Remember, though, that too many notes on the page of Scripture tend to confine your thoughts to old meditations. Alongside of your Bible have a notebook and pen to record nuggets of truth that God gives you. Jot down the date, the Scripture reading, the text, and a few thoughts—something you will never regret, especially as you reflect upon them in future days.

B. A Prayer List

preferably a looseleaf notebook so that you can always insert new pages. Put down the prayer requests of your

church, your friends, also the requests that are on your
heart. Here is a prayer cycle that you can use:

Monday: "M" is for missionaries.
Tuesday: "T" is for thanksgiving. That's when we
give the Lord special thanks for wonder-
ful answers to prayer.
Wednesday: "W" is for Christian workers.
Thursday: "T" is for tasks—the ministry God has
given.
Friday: "F" is for our families.
Saturday: "S" is for the saints—especially young
Christians, that Christ may be formed in
them.
Sunday: "S" is for sinners, and, in particular, the
gospel outreach in which we are involved.

C. A Quiet Place

With many this may be impossible at home. Such
people may want to use a nearby church, library, or
some unused room, for an hour before business, or during lunchtime. Where there's a will, there's a way. In
the summer, nothing is better than having one's quiet
time in the park, under a shady tree. Remember that
Jesus had nowhere to lay his head: he had no home of
his own, but he never missed his quiet time—never!
(see Mark 1:35). Find a place without distraction to be
totally alone with God.

D. A Definite Time

Most people agree that the morning is best, but this
may not always be possible. A time should be fixed,
however, and the appointment with the Lord punctu-
ally kept. The devil will see to it that the man of God
never drifts into having a regular devotional period. It is
imperative, therefore, that the place and time be

arranged in the presence of the Lord and then jealously guarded above everything else.

E. An Expectant Spirit

The man of God receives what he expects in his quiet time. Such an attitude is usually determined by three factors:

1. A PHYSICAL ONE

You cannot keep late hours at night and expect to be fresh to meet with God in the morning (see 1 Cor. 9:27). Your life must be strictly disciplined, if you are going to get the maximum blessing out of your daily devotions.

2. A MORAL ONE

The Word says, "If I regard iniquity in my heart, The Lord will not hear" (Ps. 66:18). This emphasizes the need for holiness. If you look with approval on anything out of adjustment to the will of God you have wrecked your quiet time. Therefore, see that your life is morally clean—nothing between yourself and your brother. If there is, make it right and then come and offer your gift of prayer and meditation (see Matt. 5:23–24).

3. A SPIRITUAL ONE

This is the need for obedience. God conditions the revelation of truth on implicit obedience. Jesus declared: "If anyone wants to do [God's] will, he shall know concerning the doctrine, whether it is from God . . ." (John 7:17). As I obey, so God reveals; as I disobey, so God ceases to reveal. Or to put it another way, "Light received bringeth light; light rejected bringeth night." Obedience and revelation go hand in hand.

III. The Regulations for the Quiet Time

Once again, these are by way of suggestion. There are seven regulations which aid the believer in the quiet place of communion with God. Let me state them simply:

A. Waiting

Samuel Chadwick says in his book on prayer that "hurry is the death of prayer." Five minutes in quiet waiting upon God will yield far more than thirty hurried minutes. Silently wait on God to realize his presence. Seek cleansing, the power of concentration, and the illumination of the Spirit. Don't even open your Bible at this point. Just wait on God and be still.

Illustration

It is said that a piano can go out of tune by hard use. The constant striking of the strings may loosen them, and they need to be adjusted if they are to continue producing harmonious sounds. Someone has written, "In like manner all common experiences have an exhausting effect on us, even when we serve the Lord. . . . As we minister to others, as we strive and struggle, duty drains our life-fountain. We then need to come into God's presence for spiritual renewal. . . . In the quietness of that fellowship he tunes our lives and strengthens us for further service.[2]

B. Reading

Now open your Bible and begin to read the portion for the day. System and sequence must be observed. Plan your reading passage by passage. The whole value of Bible reading is lost with the "lucky dip" method of reading. A short portion well read is better than a chapter or more skimped.

Illustration

When I Read the Bible Through

I supposed I knew my Bible, reading piecemeal, hit or
  miss—
Now a bit of John or Matthew, now a snatch of Genesis;
Certain chapters of Isaiah, certain Psalms (the 23rd);
12th of Romans, 1st of Proverbs. Yes, I thought I knew
  the Word.
But I found a thorough reading was a different thing to
  do,
And the way was unfamiliar when I read my Bible
  through.
You who like to play at Bible, dip and dabble here and
  there
Just before you kneel aweary and yawn out a hurried
  prayer;
You who treat the Crown of Writing as you treat no other
  book,
Just a paragraph disjointed, just a quick impatient look;
Try a worthier procedure, try a broad and steady view;
You will kneel in very rapture, when you read your Bible
  through.[3]

C. Meditating

As you read, ask yourself: Is there a promise to claim,
a lesson to learn, a blessing to enjoy, a command to obey,
a sin to avoid; a new revelation of God, Christ, the Holy
Spirit; a new thought about the devil? Such meditation,
under the control of the Holy Spirit, never fails to yield
some message to the soul.

D. Recording

Psychologists state that there is no impression without
expression. It is well to test and confirm God-given
impressions by expressing them on paper. Briefly record
the thoughts gleaned in a personal and devotional form,

and recognize that such thoughts, as illuminated by the Holy Spirit, are the spoken Word of God to your soul.

E. Praying

At this point turn the meditation into prayer and do it in this fashion: personal examination—let it search your heart. Then spiritual adoration. Praise God—even if he has rebuked you. Then turn it into general intercession. This will deliver you from stereotyped praying. Pray back to God what he has given to you until your will has been adjusted to all that the Holy Spirit has revealed to you.

F. Sharing

Leave the place of prayer determined to share the good of your quiet time with someone else during the day. As you do so it becomes doubly enriching. Not to use what the Lord has given is merely to acquire knowledge which puffs up. When the Israelites hoarded the manna during their wilderness journey, they found that it bred worms and stank. You don't lose by sharing, you gain.

G. Obeying

Rise from your knees with a determination to put into action what God has taught you.

Illustration

When Major C. H. Malan was a young officer in India, a Christian lady wrote to him, asking him to read and pray over his Bible. He did so and it led to his conversion. Writing later, he said, "Herein I was helped by being a soldier, for I began to read my Bible as I read the Queen's regulations, as if all its instructions were intended to be followed out."

Conclusion

The barometer of one's Christian life is the quiet time.
Do you have a quiet time, or have you let it slip? Be the
man of God who takes time to be holy, speaks oft with his
Lord, abides in him only, and feeds on his Word. God grant
that this may be true of you.

Believers' Baptism
Matthew 28:16–20

"Go therefore and make disciples of all the nations, baptizing them . . ." (28:19).

Introduction

The practice of believers' baptism is not exclusive to Baptist churches; it is New Testament doctrine. Much controversy has raged over the mode of baptism, but baptism is the right of every believer. This position is strengthened by the command of the Lord Jesus Christ who said, ". . . *All authority has been given to me in heaven and on earth. Go therefore and make disciples of all the nations, baptizing them in the name of the Father and of the Son and of the Holy Spirit" (28:18–19).* Observe:

I. The Institution of Believers' Baptism

"Go therefore and make disciples of all the nations, baptizing them . . ." (28:19). With these words Jesus instituted believers' baptism. The word *baptism* occurs a number of times in the New Testament without reference to believers' baptism. For instance, we read of:

A. The Baptism of Moses

"Moreover, brethren, I do not want you to be unaware that all our fathers were under the cloud, all passed through the sea, all were baptized into Moses in the cloud and in the sea" (1 Cor. 10:1–2). Paul is illustrating here how the children of Israel were identified with their leader Moses. When passing through the Red Sea on dry ground, they were covered with a cloud and flanked on either side by water—a picture of baptism.

B. The Baptism of John

"I indeed baptize you with water unto repentance, but he who is coming after me is mightier than I, whose sandals I am not worthy to carry. He will baptize you with the Holy Spirit and fire" (Matt. 3:11). This was known as the baptism of repentance. It was possible to have been baptized unto repentance and yet not to have received the Holy Spirit. When Paul went to Ephesus as a missionary he found twelve disciples who had been baptized unto the baptism of John [the Baptist]. They had repented of their sins, but had never believed in the name of Jesus, nor had they received the Holy Spirit (see Acts 19:1–5). They did not know there was such a Person—so were evidently not regenerated. After hearing of Christ Jesus and believing on him, ". . . they were baptized in the name of the Lord Jesus" (Acts 19:5) and received the manifestations of the indwelling Holy Spirit.

C. The Baptism of Jesus

Though John the Baptist baptized him, Jesus did not have to repent, for he had no sins to confess. Yet he stepped into the waters of Jordan to identify himself with his messianic mission, and to fulfill every demand of his Father (see Matt. 3:15). In a sense, if there were nothing else in all the Scriptures concerning baptism, this verse would be sufficient to encourage us to follow Jesus Christ all the way.

D. The Baptism of the Cross

Contemplating the darkness of Calvary, Jesus said, ". . . I have a baptism to be baptized with, and how distressed I am till it is accomplished" (Luke 12:50). In that midday midnight, the fountains of God's holy wrath against sin were broken up and our Savior was immersed in death for our salvation (see 2 Cor. 5:21).

E. The Baptism of the Holy Spirit

That happened at Pentecost, when the Holy Spirit was poured out by the risen Lord in accordance with the promise of the Father. The 120 disciples gathered in the upper room (and, potentially, the entire church throughout the centuries) was immersed into the one body. Paul, looking back, says, ". . . by one Spirit we were all baptized into one body . . ." (1 Cor. 12:13). John Stott points out that this baptism is once and for all, and is synonymous with our incorporation into the body of Christ.[1] Dr. C. I. Scofield affirms that there is "one baptism, many fillings, constant anointing."

F. The Baptism of Judgment

John the Baptist spoke of it: ". . . He will baptize you with the Holy Spirit [Pentecost] and fire [coming judgment]" (Matt. 3:11). Let no one think that this world is going on indefinitely. God is going to break into history again. Just as he broke into history in grace, the next time he is coming in judgment (see Acts 17:31). That is going to be a baptism of fire, when the chaff will be burned with unquenchable fire.

Illustration

In Warren Wiersbe's *Meet Yourself in the Psalms,* he tells about a frontier town where a horse bolted and ran away with a wagon carrying a little boy. Seeing the child in danger, a young man risked his life to catch the horse and stop the wagon. The child who was saved grew up to become a lawless man, and one day he stood before a judge to be sentenced for a serious crime. The prisoner recognized the judge as the man who, years before, had saved his life; so he pled for mercy on the basis of that experience. But the words from the bench silenced his plea. "Young man, then I was your savior; today I am your judge, and I must sentence you to be hanged." One day Jesus Christ will say to rebellious sinners, "During that long day of grace I was the Savior, and I would have forgiven you. But today I am your Judge. Depart from me, ye cursed, into everlasting fire!"[2]

G. The Baptism of Believers

It is the Savior who instituted believers' baptism when he said, ". . . All authority has been given to me in heaven and on earth . . . make disciples . . . baptizing them in the name of the Father and of the Son and of the Holy Spirit" (Matt. 28:19).

II. The Implication of Believers' Baptism

When a man or woman, boy or girl, is baptized, they publicly confess two things:

A. Acceptance of Christ as Savior

". . . Go into all the world and preach the gospel to every creature. He who believes and is baptized will be saved; but he who does not believe will be condemned" (Mark 16:15–16). Our salvation is dependent upon believing, not necessarily on baptism. Baptism is the outward expression of this inward transaction. The penitent thief on the cross believed and was taken to paradise by the Lord who saved him, but he was not baptized. Baptism is the public confession of having accepted Christ as personal Savior.

B. Allegiance to Christ as Lord

"Go therefore and make disciples of all the nations, baptizing them . . ." (28:19). Where there is discipleship there is lordship. There is no such thing as discipline without a master. At baptism we make known the fact that we have received Christ as Savior; we show to angels, principalities, and powers that we have acknowledged Christ as Sovereign. The Lord Jesus is looking for disciples, not names on church rolls or decision cards, but those who will own him as lord and master.

Illustration

Thomas Barclay labored for sixty years on Formosa as a missionary to the Chinese. Behind that life of service lay a covenant with God which he wrote when he was 16, and which he renewed every year. It read in part: "This day do I, with the utmost solemnity, surrender myself to Thee. I renounce all former lords that have had dominion over me, and I consecrate to Thee all that I have: the faculties of my mind, the members of my body, my worldly possessions, my time, and my influence over others; to be all used entirely for Thy glory, and resolutely employed in obedience to Thy commands, as long as Thou continuest me in life; with an ardent desire and humble resolution to continue Thine through all the ages of eternity; ever holding myself in an attentive posture to observe, with zeal and joy, to the immediate execution of it. To Thy direction also I resign myself, and all that I am and have, to be disposed of by Thee in such a manner as Thou in Thine infinite wisdom shall judge most subservient to the purposes of Thy glory. To Thee I leave the management of all events, and say without reserve, 'Not my will, but Thine, be done.'"[3]

III. The Interpretation of Believers' Baptism

"Go therefore and make disciples of all the nations, baptizing them in the name of the Father and of the Son and of the Holy Spirit, *teaching them to observe all things that I have commanded you . . .*" (28:19–20). The disciples learned quite a lot while they were with the master, but there was a great deal they did not know until after he had ascended to heaven and the Holy Spirit had come down to interpret the deeper meaning of this wonderful ordinance of believers' baptism (such as Rom. 6). Look at:

A. *Its Mention in the New Testament*

There are some doctrines for which we contend earnestly, yet they are mentioned only meagerly in the New Testament. But baptism is enjoined in the Gospels, exemplified in the Acts, and explained in the Epistles:

1. ENJOINED IN THE GOSPELS

The Great Commission (see Matt. 28:19; Mark 16). Even though the latter is a disputed passage, it is supported by such great expositors as G. Campbell Morgan and F. F. Bruce.

2. EXEMPLIFIED IN THE ACTS

The Day of Pentecost (2:41)
The Baptism of the Eunuch (8:36–38)
The Baptism of Saul of Tarsus (9:18)
The Baptism of Cornelius (10:47–48)
The Baptism of Lydia (16:15)
The Baptism of the Philippian jailer (16:33)
The Baptism of the Twelve at Ephesus (19:5)

3. Explained in the Epistles

(See Romans 6.) This is the greatest chapter on baptism in the New Testament. The teaching is simple, yet profound; simple, because baptism is intended to show us what God has done in Christ in identifying us with his death, burial, and resurrection; profound, because it is one of the great theological passages in Scripture on our union with Christ.

B. Its Method in the New Testament

The word *baptism* is a transliteration from the Greek *baptizō* meaning "to make whelmed" (i.e., fully wet) or "to dip." It was used by the Greeks in the dyeing of a garment where immersion, submersion, and emergence are inferred. Anglican Bishop Ryle points out that baptism loses all its significance if we do not see those three acts: death is down—immersion; burial is under—submersion; resurrection is out of—emergence. This is all made clear in Romans 6. The two outstanding examples of the verb *baptizo* are the baptism of our Lord in the river Jordan, not in the temple courts (see Matt. 3:16–17), and the Ethiopian eunuch (see Acts 8:38). Both he and Philip ". . . went down *into the water, and . . .* came up . . . *out of the water. . . .*"

C. Its Meaning in the New Testament

This can be set out in three very significant thoughts.

1. The Believer's Obedience to Christ

Jesus said, "Go . . . make disciples . . . baptizing them . . . and . . . teaching them to observe all things that I have commanded you . . ." (Matt. 28:19–20). There is only one response of a yielded Christian to a command: obedience. Jesus said, "If you love me, keep my commandments" (John 14:15; see also Luke

6:46). When we disobey an express command of our
Lord our spiritual growth is stunted, and God will not
reveal anything more until we obey. John writes, "If
anyone wants to do [God's] will, he shall know concerning the doctrine" (John 7:17). And the prophet
Samuel declared: ". . . to obey is better than sacrifice,
and to heed than the fat of rams" (1 Sam. 15:22). There
is no substitute for obedience. "Defective obedience
is total disobedience" (Dr. William Fitch). The Bible
says, ". . . whoever shall keep the whole law, and yet
stumble in one point, he is guilty of all" (James 2:10).

Illustration

A well-known preacher had a brother who was a famous
physician. One day a woman, wishing to speak with the
minister but not being sure if the man she was about to
address was the preacher or the physician, asked, "Are
you the doctor who preaches, or the one who practices?"
The words were a goad to the man of God, stirring his con-
science. Ever afterward he endeavored not only to hear the
Word of God and speak it, but also to do it.[4]

2. THE BELIEVER'S ONENESS WITH CHRIST

Baptism symbolizes the believer's oneness with
Christ in death, burial, and resurrection. In baptism,
the believer shows outwardly that he was crucified,
judicially, with Christ 2000 years ago; therefore, he
is dead to sin and self. Experientially, the Holy Spirit
makes that real to him (see Rom. 8:13).

The believer is also buried with Christ. What is
dead must be buried, put out of sight. And if sin and
self have been buried, then the believer has no right to
visit the cemetery and dig up those bones, represent-
ing the flesh, and allow them to paralyze his spiritual walk (see Rom. 6:1–23).

Then there is the believer's oneness with Christ in
resurrection. The only grounds on which the Holy
Spirit releases the resurrection life of Jesus, in and
through a child of God, is when he has accepted, by

faith, his place in death and burial (see Rom. 6:11; Col. 3:1–3).

3. The Believer's Offering for Christ

This ordinance is a beautiful figure of a life yielded to another. The person baptized hands himself over to the one who baptizes. This symbolizes the offering of ourselves to Christ. It must be a complete sacrifice (see Rom. 6:13; 12:1), an act of obedience, a public demonstration of our total dedication to Christ without reserve—spirit, soul, and body.

Illustration

In the "horse and buggy" days a man and his wife were driving along a narrow and dangerous road. The woman became extremely nervous, and in her fright she grabbed one of the reins. As calmly as possible the husband responded by offering her the other strap, "Oh, no!" she cried, "I don't want them both! I could never manage that animal alone!" "Well, then," he said gently, "you must make your choice. It's either you or me. We can't both drive the same horse." The frightened soul quickly surrendered full control of the wagon to her husband. Everything was once again in good hands, and they journeyed on safely. Similarly, we must turn the "reins" of our life over to Christ and let him take full control.[5]

Conclusion

We have seen what is meant by believers' baptism in terms of its mention, method, and meaning. What hinders *you* to be baptized? Will you go all the way with Jesus?

> Trust and obey,
>   for there's no other way
> To be happy in Jesus,
>   But to trust and obey
>   John H. Sammis

Church Membership

Romans 12:1–13

> ". . . we, being many, are one body in Christ, and individually members of one another" (12:5).

Introduction

We often use the opening verses of this chapter to challenge *individual* believers to a life of surrender. But to be fair to the context, we must observe that Paul is addressing the saints at Rome both personally and corporately. Here Paul is dealing with:

I. The Basis for Church Membership

"I beseech you therefore brethren, by the mercies of God, that you present your bodies a living sacrifice, holy, acceptable to God, which is your reasonable service. And do not be conformed to this world, but be transformed by the renewing of your mind, that you may prove what is that good and acceptable and perfect will of God" (12:1–2). Paul assumes that his readers had experienced the justifying and sanctifying mercies of God; this is the basis of his appeal. But in order to enjoy the harmony and ministry of a local church there are certain fundamental requirements that must be obeyed:

A. The Dedication of Our Bodies to God

"I beseech you therefore, brethren, by the mercies of God, that you present your bodies a living sacrifice, holy, acceptable to God, which is your reasonable service" (12:1). This is not something naive or nebulous. Paul beseeches the saints at Rome—and Christians throughout the centuries—to be totally, worthily, and sensibly dedicated. His appeal calls for:

B. The Transformation of Our Souls by God

"And do not be conformed to this world, but be transformed by the renewing of your mind . . ." (12:2). The Bible reminds us that ". . . as [a man] thinks in his heart, so is he . . ." (Prov. 23:7). God starts with the mind in order to affect the life. There is a twofold thrust in his appeal: first, the refusal of worldliness—". . . do not be conformed to this world . . . ," and then the renewal of holiness—". . . be transformed by the renewing of your mind . . ." (12:2).

C. The Satisfaction of Our Spirits in God

". . . that you may prove what is that good and acceptable and perfect will of God" (12:2). When there is the true dedication of our bodies to God, and the transformation of our souls by God, there follows the satisfaction of our spirits in God. There is no more satisfying place on earth than the center of God's ". . . good and acceptable and perfect will . . ." (12:2). The will of God is good because it is profitable, it is acceptable because it is pleasurable, and it is perfect because it is purposeful.

Find a group of Christians who know this dedication, transformation, and satisfaction in their lives and you will find a basis for oneness.

II. The Beauty of Our Oneness

"For I say, through the grace given to me, to everyone who is among you, not to think of himself more highly than he ought to think, but to think soberly, as God has dealt to each one a measure of faith. . . . distributing to the needs of the saints, given to hospitality" (12:3–13). These eleven verses are full of truth concerning the beauty of our membership, stewardship, and fellowship in Christ.

A. The Beauty of Our Membership

"For I say through the grace given to me, to everyone who is among you, not to think of himself more highly than he ought to think, but to think soberly, as God has dealt to each one a measure of faith. . . . [for] we, being many, are one body in Christ, and individually members of one another" (12:3, 5). Paul teaches here that if we are to know the true significance of our membership in the local church we must recognize two important things:

1. OUR INDIVIDUAL MODESTY

". . .everyone . . . is . . . not to think of himself more highly than he ought to think, but to think soberly, as God has dealt to each one a measure of faith" (12:3). Here he warns against self-exaltation—thinking of ourselves more highly than ". . . we ought to think. . . ." He also warns against self-depreciation (implied in thinking "soberly"). Instead, we are to seek self-realization, ". . . as God has dealt to each one a measure of faith" (12:3). There is a redeemed and released self that the Holy Spirit wants to use for the glory of God. This is Christian modesty. Once we recognize that God does not make duplicates, but only originals, then we shall realize the purpose for which he has saved and separated us for his service and glory.

Illustration

The three smallest bones in the human body—the malleus, incus, and the stapes—are located in the middle ear. Only when they are in proper functioning order is hearing possible.

A surgeon performed an operation (a stapedectomy) on the third smallest of these bones for a man who had not heard anything in 26 years. The patient was under partial anesthesia, and as the surgeon was about to join the bones, he said, "Howie, keep talking as I join the bones and keep your eyes on me." The instant the surgeon joined those bones, the man's eyes got big as saucers. "W-s-what's that? Who's talking? Why, that's me! That's my voice I hear!" Tears streamed down the man's face, and a nurse wiped them away with some gauze.

In the body of Christ, size does not determine the significance of the members. A Christian may belittle himself because he's not an "arm," but he may be as a "stapes" for clearly transmitting communications. Why? Because he is an essential part of the body.[1]

2. Our Interpersonal Unity

"For as we have many members in one body, but all the members do not have the same function, so we, being many, are one body in Christ, and individually members of one another" (12:4–5). As individuals, we are part of a whole. In Jesus Christ, the church is an indivisible unity (see 12:4a). Even though there are human divisions and factions, God

sees us as one. Therefore, there is nothing more serious than rending the seamless robe of Christ.

But more than this, in Jesus Christ we are an indispensable unity—". . . we, being many, are one body in
Christ, and individually members of one another"
(12:5). We need each other. The eye can't say to the
nose, "I have no need of you." The ear can't say to
the mouth, "I have no need of you." The hand can't
say to the foot, "I have no need of you" (see 1 Cor.
12:12–31). All are indispensable to one another, and
therefore interdependent.

Illustration

Specialists have wondered why Canadian geese always
fly in a "V" formation, so their engineers did a study on
the subject. They discovered that the flapping of each
goose's wings provided an upward lift for the goose that
followed. When all the geese were flying in perfect formation, the whole flock had a 71 percent greater flying range
than if each bird flew alone. Each was dependent on the
other to reach its destination. Likewise, the church needs
to learn that it's at least 71 percent easier to live the Christian life by "flying with the flock" than it is to fly alone.

B. The Beauty of Our Stewardship (see 12:6–8)

In these verses Paul details seven different forms of
stewardship which operate within the local church (the
very number suggests perfect harmony). No believer
with a Christlike estimate of himself and others can set
one gift over against another, and so spoil the relation-
ships of the church by jealousy or pride. Paul distinctly
says, "Having . . . gifts differing according to the grace
. . . given to us, let us use them . . ." (12:6). This means
that every believer has a gift, yet no Christian has all
the gifts. Consider these seven aspects of stewardship:

1. THE STEWARDSHIP OF PREACHING

". . . if prophecy, let us prophesy in proportion to our faith" (12:6). This is the gift of inspired preaching. It is forthtelling rather than foretelling. Paul defines prophecy in 1 Corinthians 14:3 where he says: ". . . he who prophesies speaks edification and exhortation and comfort to men." Such a ministry builds up, stirs up, and cheers up the church.

2. THE STEWARDSHIP OF SERVING

". . . or ministry, let us use it in our ministering" (12:7). This is business and administrative service in the life of the church, though not always limited to mundane and material matters (see Acts 6:1, 4). Both the distribution of money, food, and the preaching of the Word were performed by Spirit-filled deacons.

3. THE STEWARDSHIP OF TEACHING

". . . he who teaches, in teaching" (12:7). This is the gift of exposition and interpretation. Priscilla and Aquila possessed this gift; for example, they detected a lack of teaching in the preaching of Apollos. Taking him aside, they ". . . explained to him the way of God more accurately" (Acts 18:26).

4. THE STEWARDSHIP OF HELPING

". . . he who exhorts, in exhortation" (12:8). This word literally means "consolation," "encouragement," and even "challenge." Exhortation can be used two ways: it can spur people or woo them. Basically, it is a ministry of helping to apply what has already been taught, though it is distinct from the gift of teaching.

5. THE STEWARDSHIP OF GIVING

". . . he who gives, with liberality . . ." (12:8). This is the gift of liberality and stewardship in money. There is a sense in which all believers possess this gift to a greater or lesser degree. The ministry of sharing should be exercised with singleness of heart and cheerfulness of spirit ". . . for God loves a cheerful giver" (2 Cor. 9:7).

6. THE STEWARDSHIP OF LEADING

". . . he who leads, with diligence . . ." (12:8). This gift of leadership can be applied to organizers, superintendents, or directors of Christian work. In the New Testament, it applies to family life (see 1 Thess. 5:12; 1 Tim. 3:4), and also describes the office of the elder (see 1 Tim. 5:17). Such leadership must be exercised with diligence.

7. THE STEWARDSHIP OF CARING

". . . he who shows mercy, with cheerfulness" (12:8). This is the gift of pastoral visitation. It includes the care of the sick, the poor, the afflicted, and the sorrowing, and is to be carried out with cheerfulness (or hilarity). It requires a sense of humor born of Holy Spirit joy. This verse could be paraphrased as follows: "If you come to sympathize and sorrow, bring God's sunlight in your face."

Illustration

A Smile

It needs so little sympathy to cheer a weary way,
Sometimes a little kindness lights up a dreary day;
A very simple, friendly word may hope and strength impart,
Or just an understanding smile revive some fainting heart;
And, like a sudden sunlit ray, lighting a darkened room,
A sunny spirit may beguile the deepest depths of gloom.

C. The Beauty of Our Fellowship (see 12:9–13)

The key verse is verse 9: "Let love be without hypocrisy . . ." A hypocrite originally meant "the stage player" who acted his part but was not real. So the apostle exhorts, "Don't play at church, but be real in your fellowship of love." Paul then outlines the characteristics of love.

1. A LOVE WHICH IS PURE

". . . Abhor what is evil. Cling to what is good" (12:9). Dr. Graham Scroggie once said, "True love is not present where there is not a moral recoil from evil." True love should bind us to that which is good, and there is a sense in which evil will be abhorred in exact proportion to one's adherence to that which is good.

2. A LOVE WHICH IS PERSONAL

"Be kindly affectionate to one another with brotherly love, in honor giving preference to one another" (12:10; see also 1 John 3:14). True love seeks out individuals and loves them personally. It is a love which gives recognition and honor to all Christians, without respect of persons.

3. A LOVE WHICH IS PASSIONATE

". . . not lagging in diligence, fervent in spirit, serving the Lord" (12:10). These three exhortations are closely connected. The Christian must be zealous in all he seeks to do for the glory of God and the good of man. The whole thought in this verse is that of a passionate love for the Lord Jesus in every aspect of Christian service.

4. A LOVE WHICH IS POSITIVE

". . . rejoicing in hope . . ." (12:12). Whatever the circumstances of life, love is always radiantly optimistic. Storms may come and go, but the anchor of hope remains sure and steadfast because it is grounded in God's love. Hallelujah for a love which is positive!

5. A LOVE WHICH IS PATIENT

". . . patient in tribulation . . ." (12:12). Whatever the frustrations or persecutions, the believers is to *endure*—a needed quality in Christian life and service. We live in such days of busyness, hurry, and pressure that we have lost the art of being patient.

Illustration

When J. Hudson Taylor was asked what he considered to be the three greatest qualities for a missionary, he replied: "The first is patience, the second is patience, and the third is patience."

6. A LOVE WHICH IS PRAYERFUL

". . . continuing steadfastly in prayer" (12:12). This exhortation refers to the Christian's activity and attitude of prayer. Such prayerfulness keeps all other expressions of love in a state of health. The effect of such prayerfulness in the life of the church is beyond computation. It is only when people come together in prayer that the fellowship of love is strengthened and deepened.

7. A LOVE WHICH IS PRACTICAL

". . . distributing to the needs of the saints, given to hospitality" (12:13). This is love in action, not just in word. John writes in his epistle: ". . . whoever has this world's goods, and sees his brother in need, and shuts up his heart from him, how does the love of God abide in him?" (1 John 3:17). True love communicates to the necessity of the saints in practical benevolence; it provides hospitality. The word "given" to hospitality is the same as that which is translated "to pursue," or "to follow after" (see Phil. 3:6, 12, 14). Paul personifies love as it pursues lonely souls in a loveless world in order that they might be given the hospitality of Christian fellowship. The same thought occurs in Hebrews 13:1–2—"Let brotherly love continue. Do not forget to entertain strangers, for by so doing some have unwittingly entertained angels."

Illustration

"Old Bill" was hired to sweep streets in a small town in the hills. He was a friendly old fellow, and Miss Gidding who lived in the corner house got into the habit all that summer of taking him a glass of lemonade and a slice of cake. He thanked her shyly and that was all. One evening there was a knock at the back door of Miss Gidding's house. Bill was there with a sack of peaches in one arm and a handful of corn in the other. He seemed embarrassed as he said, "I brought you these, Ma'am, for your kindness." "Oh, you shouldn't have," she replied, "it was nothing." "Maybe it wasn't much, Ma'am," he answered, "but it was more than anyone else did."

How can we know the love of God in our lives? Paul gives the secret. He says in Romans 5:5, ". . . the love of God has been poured out in our hearts by the Holy Spirit who was given to us." To know the release of this love we must remove the limitations that prevent the flow of the Spirit in our lives (ignorance, prejudice, unbelief). Then we must renew the obligations that promote the flow of the Spirit in our lives. This involves obedience (see Acts 5:32) and faith (see Luke 11:13).

Conclusion

We see, then, what we mean by church membership. The basis is clear. There must be dedication, transformation, and satisfaction in our lives. The beauty of that oneness must be expressed, by the Holy Spirit's power, through membership, stewardship, and fellowship. Only then will we know what it is to dwell together in unity (see Psalm 133:1).

10

Consecrated Living

Romans 12:1–2

"Present your bodies a living sacrifice, holy, acceptable to God, which is your reasonable service" (12:1).

Introduction

What God wants today is new men, rather than new methods; surrendered people, rather than just saved people, for it is possible to be saved yet not surrendered. The burden of the apostle Paul in this chapter—and particularly verses 1 and 2—is to show that the purpose of our salvation is that we might be truly surrendered to all the will of God. In the preceding chapters, Paul has been dealing with the salvation and sanctification of the believer's life; in these verses his theme is the surrender of the believer's life. Notice:

I. The Divine Obligation to Surrender

"I beseech you therefore, brethren, by the mercies of God, that you present your bodies a living sacrifice, holy,

acceptable to God, which is your reasonable service"
(12:1). The apostle shows us that his obligation is occasioned by:

A. The Revelation of Divine Love

"I beseech you therefore . . . by the mercies of
God . . ." (12:1). Mercy is love in action extended to an
inferior. When an inferior looks up to a superior, he recognizes that the superior is showing mercy when he
expresses love. Notice that it is "mercies" in the plural.
In the previous chapter the apostle has unveiled the
matchless mercy of God as seen in Christ. Who can
remain unmoved by the grace that has appeared to sinful men: justifying, sanctifying, and glorifying them?
Paul has described how the sinner, condemned before
God, is helpless and meritless; and how God, in the
Lord Jesus Christ, comes in grace and mercy, setting him
at liberty, and giving him justification, sanctification,
and glorification (see Rom. 3:24; 5:8, 6:23; 8:1, 29–30,
38–39).

Illustration

Richard Armstrong, *Make Your Life Worthwhile,* reports
the story about a man in Wales who sought to win the
affection of a certain lady for 42 years before she finally
said "Yes." The couple, both 74, recently became "Mr.
and Mrs." For more than 40 years, the persistent, but
rather shy man slipped a weekly love letter under his
neighbor's door. But she continually refused to speak
and mend the spat that had parted them many years
before. After writing 2,184 love letters without ever getting
a spoken or written answer, the single-hearted old man
eventually summoned up enough courage to present himself in person. He knocked on the door of the reluctant
lady's house and asked for her hand. To his delight and
surprise, she accepted. Imagine God's dilemma. Time
and time again He has tried to get His message of love
through to His human creation with little response. Finally,

when there was no other way, He wrapped up His message and came in person. What a revelation of God's love to you and me!

B. The Expectation of Divine Love

"I beseech you therefore, brethren, by the mercies of God, that you present your bodies a living sacrifice, holy, acceptable to God, which is your reasonable service" (12:1). The apostle John puts it a little differently when he says, "We love Him because He first loved us" (1 John 4:19).

True gratitude requires expression. Who can reason out the mercies of God without a deep sense of obligation to respond to these mercies? In other words, the logic of love "demands my soul, my life, my all." None of us can think of all that Christ gave at Calvary without a deep desire to say, "Lord Jesus, you have done all this for me; from now onward I will live only for you." Any person who has been saved but has never surrendered his life to Christ is one who has never given serious consideration to the love of God, as revealed in the Lord Jesus.

Illustration

An aged countryman visited London for the first time. In a great art gallery, he looked at different paintings. He was especially impressed with a picture of Christ dying on the cross. As he gazed fixedly on it, a deeper love for the Savior flooded his heart. With great feeling, he exclaimed, "Bless Him! I love Him! I love Him!" Those standing nearby heard him. They saw tears glistening on his careworn face as he stood completely oblivious of the presence of others. Four of them came close to him and said, "We, too, love Him, brother." Though strangers to each other, they were drawn together in love and adoration for the Savior.[1]

II. The Divine Order of Surrender

". . . present your bodies a living sacrifice, holy, acceptable to God . . ." (12:1). The apostle insists that the act, as well as the attitude, of surrender must be totally offered, and then worthily offered.

A. Totally Offered

". . . present your bodies . . ." (12:1). That word *present* means "yield," and suggests the handing over of a gift. It was a term used in the temple. It is the voluntary response of the believer to God's love, grace, and mercy.

Notice what we are to present: our bodies (12:1). The body here stands for the complete man, including soul and spirit. It symbolizes the giving over of everything. The body is that which God must have, if he is to express his perfect will through us to the world. He wants our brains, eyes, ears, tongue, hands, and feet as the vehicle for the divine expression.

What we do with our bodies now will determine our reward or loss in the coming day of judgment. Believers will stand before the judgment seat of Christ ". . . that each one may receive the things done in the body, according to what he has done, whether good or bad" (2 Cor. 5:10). Thank God, we are not going to be judged on the sin question; that was dealt with at Calvary, but we shall be judged for service we have rendered in the body down here on earth. So until we surrender our bodies God can never consecrate us to his service.

It is tremendously important to realize that God never consecrates part of the life, only the whole. When the high priest was consecrated, the anointing oil went from his head to his feet. It was all or nothing. So until you are prepared to surrender spirit, soul, and body upon God's altar, he cannot consecrate you. You may be saved, but you are not surrendered, or consecrated.

In the Old Testament, God had very specific instructions concerning the offering of animal sacrifices. When the priest slew them, he had to lay the pieces of their flesh on the altar with deliberateness and thoughtfulness.

Illustration

Florence Nightingale at thirty wrote in her diary, "I am thirty years of age, the age at which Christ began His mission. Now no more childish things, no more vain things. Now, Lord, let me think only of Thy will." Years later, near the end of her illustrious, heroic life she was asked for her life's secret, and she replied, "Well, I can only give one explanation; that is, I have kept nothing back from God."[2]

B. *Worthily Offered*

". . . a living sacrifice, holy, acceptable to God . . ." (12:1). This is a sacrificial phrase and carries the thought of a burnt offering, i.e., an offering wholly consumed. Notice how God insists that our offering should be brought. It should be:

1. A LIVING SACRIFICE (12:1)

Three ideas are implicit in that word *living*. To be "a living sacrifice," it has to be *intelligently alive*. The offerer and the sacrifice are one and the same person, which is a complete contrast to the animal sacrifices of the Old Testament (they did not know what was happening). You and I must know what we are doing as we present our offering. What is more, our offering must be *spiritually alive*. An unconverted person can never offer anything to God; he can only receive from God. That is why our emphasis is always that a person who is "dead in trespasses and sins" (Eph. 2:1) must acknowledge his sinnership and pray:

> Just as I am, without one plea,
> But that Thy blood was shed for me,

And that Thou bidd'st me come to Thee,
O Lamb of God, I come! . . .

Charlotte Elliot

Only when a person is truly converted does he qual-
ify to bring something to God; he must be indwelt by
the life-giving Spirit.

Furthermore, God insists that our offering must be
continually alive. When the Old Testament priest slew
the animal on the north side of the altar, and placed it
upon the altar, he knew it must be kept there until it
was wholly consumed. So often with a big sacrifice
there was the tendency for it to slip off the altar. God
foresaw that and instructed Moses and Aaron that
they should use fleshhooks (see Exod. 27:3), which
were part of the furniture of the tabernacle, to bring
the sacrifice back to the center of the flame.

Here is a message for you and me. When we yield
our spirit, soul, and body to God, there is the tendency, again and again, to slip from the place of surrender. When that happens we need to use those
fleshhooks of determination and discipline to bring
us back to the center of the flame, and we will have to
do that until Jesus comes or calls.

Illustration

Stephen Olford remembers talking to a young lady who
said, "Mr. Olford, this business of consecration does not
work. Many a time I have stood up and yielded my life to the
Lord; but a few weeks later I was back where I started."
"You have never really yielded your life to the Lord," Olford
said. "New Testament surrender means that when you put
your sacrifice on the altar it is not for a day, or a month, or a
year, but forever. Tell me, what are you doing off the altar?"

2. A HOLY SACRIFICE

". . . present your bodies a . . . sacrifice, holy, . . ."
(12:1). We cannot offer to the Lord ". . . that which
costs [us] nothing . . ." (2 Sam. 24:24). In Malachi

1:7–8 we read that the people made the altar of the Lord contemptible, and offered the blind for sacrifice. In God's eyes it was evil and defiled. When God asks for a holy sacrifice he means a sacrifice which has been *initially* cleansed by the precious blood of Christ and then *continually* cleansed by the daily application of the Word of God to our lives.

3. A PLEASING SACRIFICE

"Present your bodies a . . . sacrifice . . . acceptable to God . . ." (12:1). To the apostle, the word "acceptable" would be associated with what is known as the ascending offering. Whether seen or unseen to the public eye, the sacrifice had to be pleasing.

Similarly, the believer must please God in private and public life. How true this was of the Lord Jesus! As a boy, he said, ". . . I must be about My Father's business" (Luke 2:49). And when he stood on the banks of Jordan, at the age of 30, and was baptized, a voice was heard from heaven, saying "This is My beloved Son, in whom I am well pleased" (Matt. 3:17). There are many Christians who look like saints in public, but act like demons in private. We must please God at all times, if our surrender is to be real and sincere.

III. The Divine Object in Surrender

". . . do not be conformed to this world, but be transformed by the renewing of your mind, that you may prove what is that good and acceptable and perfect will of God" (12:2). The object of the believer's surrender is twofold:

A. The Transformation of the Believer's Character

". . . do not be conformed to this world, but be transformed by the renewing of your mind . . ." (12:2). As the believer maintains an attitude of surrender, a daily change takes place in the life, which is here described both negatively and positively.

Negatively, it means nonconformity to the world (see 12:2). To be conformed means to be like, or to take the shape of. The surrendered believer is no longer conformed to the policies, fashions, and practices of the world about him; there is a distinctiveness and difference of lifestyle that sets him apart from the natural and carnal man. So many Christians are like chameleons that change their color according to their surroundings: you cannot tell the difference between them and the unconverted. That is one of the biggest stumbling blocks to the witness of the Christian church.

Positively, it is to be transformed in character. God's redemptive purpose for each one of us is to be like his Son. This is the reason why he has chosen and called us.

Illustration

On a wall near the main entrance to the Alamo in San Antonio, Texas, is a portrait with the following inscription: "James Butler Bonham—no picture of him exists. This portrait is of his nephew, Major James Bonham, deceased, who greatly resembled his uncle. It is placed here by the family that people may know the appearance of the man who died for freedom." No literal portrait of Jesus exists either. But the likeness of the Son who makes us free can be seen in the lives of his true followers.[3]

Conformity to Christ takes place when the believer is yielded, fulfilling the divine order of surrender day by day. So we are changed ". . . from glory to glory, just as by the Spirit of the Lord" (2 Cor. 3:18). One of the greatest thrills for a pastor is to see almost a facial, external change coming over a person—an index to the inner change of character. That is why the hymn is so true.

What a wonderful change in my life has been wrought
Since Jesus came into my heart![4]

B. The Regulation of the Believer's Conduct

". . . that you may prove what is that good and acceptable and perfect will of God" (12:2). There is no greater joy on earth or in heaven than the realization of the will of God, and you can never be in the center of his will until you are a yielded Christian. God's will is *good;* that is, it is beneficial in its effect upon us. Therefore, we need never fear the consequences of obeying God. God's will is *acceptable*, or pleasing. It is never irksome or grievous (see 1 John 5:3). God's will is *perfect*; that is, flawless and mature. In his Sermon on the Mount, Jesus said, "you shall be perfect, just as your Father in heaven is perfect" (Matt. 5:48). The only way to be perfect in condition—and one day in consummation—is to be a yielded Christian.

Conclusion

We have seen that if a life is truly surrendered, it is to be a living, holy, and acceptable sacrifice, evidenced not only in the transformation of character, but the regulation of conduct. May we know in experience the divine obligation to surrender, the divine order of surrender, and the divine object in surrender, and so be able to say:

> Savior, Thy dying love Thou gavest me,
> Nor should I ought withhold, Dear Lord, from Thee:
> In love my soul would bow, My heart fulfill its vow,
> Some offering bring Thee now, Something for Thee.
> Sylvanus D. Phelps

Can you change that last line and say, "My ALL for Thee"? Remember, he consecrates only the whole.

11

Systematic Giving

2 Corinthians 9:5–11;
1 Corinthians 16:1–2

". . . enriched in everything for all liberality, which causes thanksgiving through us to God" (9:11).

Introduction

Can a Christian give sacrificially and save money? The answer will be given in the unfolding of our message; but suffice it to say that this subject is of the utmost importance to all Christians.

Have you ever stopped to consider how many hours you spend, outside of sleeping and eating, in the business of making money? What we do with it, then, our approach and attitude to it, is a top priority in our thinking and living.

Of course, there can be a false motive in earning money. There is the vice which grips people's minds, and hearts, so that they burn with a passion to get rich. The apostle Paul warns young Timothy very solemnly of this when he says, ". . . the love of money is a root of all evil . . ." (1 Tim. 6:10). It can be demonstrated that practically every kind of evil can spring from the lure and lust of getting rich.

What we are concerned about now, however, is the ministry of giving. We shall think of it in three aspects:

I. The Motive in Giving

". . . enriched in everything for all liberality . . ." (9:11). The supreme motive is not "What shall I gain?" but "What shall I give?" It is not one of satisfying myself, but rather of pleasing and honoring God.

A. Pleasing God

"But do not forget to do good and to share, for with such sacrifices God is well pleased" (Heb. 13:16). If someone were to ask you, "What is the greatest ambition of your life, now that you are a Christian?" what would you say? After some thought, you would possibly reply, "My greatest ambition is to please God. I love God, I love the Lord Jesus and his Word, and I want to please him." Well, here is one way in which you can please him.

Illustration

Dr. Paul White of *Jungle Doctor* fame tells of two African lepers who were desperately eager to help the missionaries. Their hands were badly disfigured with leprosy. For several weeks they worked in the sawpit, sawing logs into boards for the extension of the bush hospital. When they were given their wages, the doctor noticed them dividing their money into two piles of silver. They explained that half was for the Lord. "But that's too much. God only asks for a tenth." "But Bwana," one of them replied quickly, "we love Him far more than that!" Here were two men who desired to please God.

B. Honoring God

"Honor the LORD with your possessions, and with the first fruits of all your increase" (Prov. 3:9). That is good Old Testament language. Remember also the word from the Old Testament which God spoke to the people: ". . . those who honor Me I will honor (1 Sam. 2:30). When we come to the New Testament, we read such verses as: "It is more blessed to give than to receive" (Acts 20:35). Next to pleasing God is honoring him with our substance. Failure to do this dishonors God.

Illustration

Mr. W. R. Spight was a wholesale grocer in Decatur, Alabama. A friend who knew him said that he gave $500 to the Lord every Sunday of the year, while he lived. The Lord has said, "Them that honor me I will honor" (1 Sam. 2:30). Only eternity will reveal the vast amount of good accomplished by his giving. What better use of money than honoring the Lord![1]

II. The Method of Giving

"'Bring all the tithes into the storehouse, That there may be food in My house, And prove Me now in this,' says the LORD of hosts, 'If I will not open for you the windows of heaven and pour out for you such blessing that there will not be room enough to receive it'" (Mal. 3:10). The method in giving concerns four sections of our income: (1) tithes; (2) offerings; (3) savings; and (4) expenses.

A. Tithes

"Bring all the tithes into the storehouse . . ." (Mal. 3:10). God demands our tithes. The tithe is one-tenth of our [gross] income. Today we think in terms of money, but in olden times it was always in terms of substance.

The tithe was spoken of long before the giving of the Law. Abraham tithed, Melchizedek tithed, Jacob tithed. God introduced this principle of tithing into the life of man right from the beginning, just as he introduced the law of rest, the Sabbath, to Adam. In the same way, the giving of the tenth was that which God built into the very moral structure of his universe. The principle of tithing goes right through Scripture, and there is nothing in the New Testament which abrogates or rescinds it. As a matter of fact, the law of grace underlines it, for grace does not make void the law: it enables us to keep the law, by the very power of the indwelling Christ. If the Jew, under law, gave a tithe, can we, under grace, give any less?

One of the key passages in Scripture concerning tithing is found in Malachi 3:10, as we have seen already. Just before that God had said to the nation, ". . . you have robbed Me!" (Mal. 3:8), and then he explains how they had robbed him: ". . . in tithes and offerings" (Mal. 3:8). Now the "storehouse," in olden times, was the temple at Jerusalem. Since Jerusalem was the city of the king, and the temple was at the heart of it, all gifts had to be brought to the one place. And sometimes cattle had to be sold for that which was cash, in order to bring it into the storehouse of God.

Paul teaches this conclusively in that first verse of 1 Corinthians 16, where he talks about laying aside that portion, which God has blessed us with, and bringing it to God. Our first responsibility, as Christian people, is to bring our tithe to the place of our "Jerusalem," our "temple"—the local church.

A tithe is something which God demands. Any Christian who withholds it is, in fact, robbing him. Our money belongs to God, even before we offer it. One of the secrets of blessing is not only the yieldedness of the life, but the givingness of the life.

Illustration

The greatest surprise of Mary's life was receiving a dollar on her fourth birthday. She carried the bill about the house and was seen sitting on the stairs admiring it. "What are you going to do with your dollar?" her mother asked. "Take it to your teacher?" Mary shook her head. "No," she said, "I'm going to give it to God. He'll be as surprised as I am to get something besides pennies."

B. Offerings

". . . enriched in everything for all liberality . . ." (9:11). If God demands our tithes, he deserves our offerings. An offering is that which is given voluntarily, over and above the tithe. That is clear from any careful study of that word "offering" throughout the Old Testament Scriptures, and particularly that passage in Malachi (3:8). It usually represents something which is extra; maybe the result of a bonus, or an increase in salary, or some unexpected windfall. Or it may be in response to some blessing God has lavished on you and you want to give him an extra thank-offering, a love offering.

That is absolutely consistent with New Testament teaching, for when Paul asked the Corinthian believers for money for the deprived saints in Jerusalem, he was asking them for the extra tithe to cover the needs there (1 Cor. 16:3).

Illustration

Pastor Howard Conaster of the 4,000 member Beverly Hills Baptist Church in Dallas once preached a series of sermons on the types of offerings in Scripture. At one midweek prayer meeting he announced that a freewill offering would be received. Normally, collections are not a part of the church's prayer meeting. Conaster told his audience of 950 that the church didn't really need the money. "We are already $100,000 over our budget for this year," he said. "But you need to be blessed; you need to experience the grace of giving." After the offering was received the pastor directed the deacons to return to the congregation with the baskets, which contained more than $1,000. "It's God's money," he explained. "If you need money and have asked God to help you get it, take what you need." Only a few did but for them the collection in reverse was a god-send, observed reporter Helen Parmley of the *Dallas Morning News*. One parishioner told of a clean but poorly dressed youth who took a couple of bills from the basket as it passed, then lifted his head and said softly, "Praise the Lord."[2]

C. Savings

God defends our savings. Drawing an illustration from nature, the apostle Paul says in 2 Corinthians 12:14: ". . . the children ought not to lay up for the parents, but the parents for the children." Everyone of us has a moral obligation in relation to finance; we should save to meet our commitments. The husband who does not save for his wife, in case anything happens to him; the parents who do not save for their children; the children who do not help their widowed mother or some other dependent, when they have the ability to do so, are all breaking a very clear injunction of Scripture. First Timothy 5:8 says: ". . . if anyone does not provide for his own, and especially for those of his household, he has denied the faith and is worse than an unbeliever." The teaching is clear: we must save in order to cover our dependents. Each one of us must think this through for ourselves.

True, some wonderful stories are told of men who have given everything to missions, and through lack of foresight and careful understanding of the Word of God, have left their wives or children without adequate provision with tragic consequences. This kind of thing does not match up with the plain, practical teaching of the Bible. We must care for our dependents.

D. Expenses

God directs our expenses. We must live within our means in order to cover all liabilities. The Word of God says, "Repay no one evil for evil. Have regard for good things in the sight of all men"; and again: "Render therefore to all their due: taxes to whom taxes are due . . . Owe no one anything . . ." (Rom. 12:17; 13:7–8). If we are living a yielded Christian life, then our expenses should be directed by God. We should be living on a level at which we can meet all our expenses. We should never undertake any project which legitimately cannot be underwritten. It does not mean that you necessarily have to pay your bills on the spot, or that you cannot borrow on the bank; it refers rather to business transactions which you know you cannot justifiably and honestly cover.

Since every power is ordained of God, we should "Render . . . to all their due . . ." (Rom. 13:7). This means paying our income tax or custom fees.

To meet our obligations it may be necessary to tighten our belts, or to seek help if we are having problems arranging our financial affairs, so that our testimony as citizens, and as Christians, is above reproach.

III. The Miracle in Giving

". . . that you, always . . . have an abundance for every good work" (9:8). God is no man's debtor. As we give in the right spirit, he blesses, and that in a twofold way:

A. Materially

". . . God is able to make all grace abound toward you, that you, always having all sufficiency in all things, have an abundance for every good work . . . enriched in everything for all liberality, which causes thanksgiving through us to God" (9:8, 11). While God blesses materially, he does not necessarily make us millionaires. There are some men and women whom God selects, because of their business skills, and uses them to produce the money for the work of the church. Even though everyone is not chosen to prosper, God will see to it that we have enough to meet our needs—if we fulfill our commitments to him. Paul had ". . . learned in whatever state [he was], to be content." He knew "how to be abased, and . . . how to abound . . ." (Phil. 4:11–12). That is the supreme secret of it all. When a man has been completely delivered from the spirit of materialism it's just as easy to be a king as to be a slave. Why? Because his contentment is in Jesus Christ.

Illustration

The history of Christian giving demonstrates that there is none so poor that he cannot give. A woman with no money was too old to work. She began to pray, "teach me to obtain. Give me someone to send out and support as a missionary." Before her death, she was supporting ninety-three missionaries!

When William Colgate left home as a boy of 16 the only trade he knew was soap and candlemaking. One day he met the captain of a canal boat who gave him this piece of advice: "Someone will soon be the leading soapmaker in New York. It can be you as well as anyone. . . . Be a good man, give your heart to Christ. Give the Lord all that belongs to Him of every dollar you earn. Make an honest soap. Give a full pound, and you will be a prosperous and rich man." On arrival in the city, he joined a church, and sought to ". . . seek first the kingdom of God and His righteousness. . ." (Matt. 6:33). As his business prospered, he gave ten cents of every dollar to the Lord, then two-tenths, rising to five-tenths. Later when his children were educated, he gave all his income, amounting to millions, to the Lord.

B. *Spiritually*

"Do not be deceived, God is not mocked; for whatever man sows, that he will also reap. For he who sows to his flesh will of the flesh reap corruption, but he who sows to the Spirit will of the Spirit reap everlasting life" (Gal. 6:7–8). We quote these verses for all manner of things. We say that if you sow a sinful life you reap a wasteful life. We speak about an individual sowing his wild oats; but primarily these words refer to giving. The Bible says, "Let him who is taught the word share in all good things with him who teaches" (Gal. 6:6). In other words, the ministers of God should be well supported. Here is one of the crying sins of our time.

Whether or not the Christian who gives to God is prospered materially, he is always prospered spiritually. We have no problem about yielding our lives to God. We have little doubt as to our church responsibilities; but so often there is a lack of teaching on this important subject of giving.

Conclusion

Remember the motive in giving. You give not to get, but because you want to please and honor God. As to the method, remember the tithe is God's. He demands it, he deserves the offering, he defends the savings, he directs the expenses. Then the miracle will happen. God will prosper you sufficiently for you to be content. He may even make you the steward of great wealth. Certainly he will bless you spiritually. Next time you sing that beautiful consecration hymn, may it be more than just words:

> Take my silver and my gold,
> Not a mite would I withhold . . .
> Frances R. Havergal

12

Dedicated Serving
Exodus 21:1–6; Romans 12:9–11

> "Not slothful in business; fervent in spirit; serving the Lord" (12:11).

Introduction

Dedicated service touches every department of our lives. Service for Jesus Christ is as much an attitude of life as it is an activity of life. Whether it be so-called full-time service, a regular secular job, or caring for the home, all should be done to the glory of God with equal efficiency and fervency. Scripture makes no distinction between so-called "full-time" service and secular work; the distinction is purely an artificial one. A housewife doing her task in the home—bringing up the children, peeling the potatoes, polishing the brass, or making the beds—serves the Lord just as much as a preacher in the pulpit, or the missionary on the foreign field, if she does her job in the power of the Holy Spirit. There are three aspects of dedicated service to which I want to draw your attention:

I. Determined Service

"Not slothful in business . . ." (12:11, KJV). Paul is calling for diligence and determination in whatever the Christian is called to do, whether he be a chimney sweep or whether he be a lecturer; whether he be a preacher or a missionary. Study the various translations and you will see that the idea of business, as such, is not necessarily in this text. A better rendering is, "Never let your zeal flag." In other words, service for the Lord Jesus Christ is not so much what you do but how you do it. Paul gives few hints in his writings as to what the Christian should do by way of service, outside of witnessing, the winning of precious souls, and the preaching of the gospel. All of life is an arena in which we witness by life and by lip, but it's how we do what we do that is all-important. This is a call to:

A. Enthusiastic Determination

"Not slothful in business . . ." (12:11, KJV). The purpose of our redemption, according to Titus 2:14, is that we might be a purified people, a special people, "zealous for good works." If you read the passage and see the whole sweep of truth, you will see that salvation and service are simultaneous in their impact upon us. The moment a man is saved he serves. Salvation and service happen together. When Saul of Tarsus was converted on the Damascus road, the first question he asked was, ". . . Lord, what do You want me to do? . . ." (Acts 9:6). And when our Lord called his disciples, he said, ". . . follow me, and I will make you fishers of men" (Matt. 4:19). The "come" of salvation and the "call" of service were married together in the master's one sentence.

It is sad to see how many people who call themselves Christians are lacking in this zeal; they have never interpreted their salvation as a total commitment to Jesus Christ, in terms of service. Given a job to do, they go about it as though it were boring and uninteresting, whereas it should be the most thrilling and fascinating thing in all the world. No Christian should face his job without asking himself, "Has God called me to do this work? Is this a vocation? Is this the purpose of God for my life?" If it is, then it's not just a job, it's a ministry; and the monotonous is transformed into the momentous. Every day becomes a glorious adventure with the Lord Jesus Christ.

Whatever our master did he did it enthusiastically and fervently, whether serving as a carpenter or carrying through his redemptive task on the way to Calvary. Indeed, he preached with such fervor, he worked so untiringly, that the disciples, on one occasion marveled at the passion with which he worked for God. Turning to them he asked, [have you never read] ". . . the zeal of thine house hath eaten me up" (John 2:17, KJV; see Ps. 69:9). It is the same word that Paul uses in Titus 2— "zealous for good works." In winning us to himself, he desires that we might have the same zeal in our service for God.

So often in Christian circles we find three kinds of people: the workers, the shirkers, and the jerkers. The *workers* are people who always have their sleeves rolled up to do a real job for God. They're at the task, whether it's snowing or the sun is shining; whether the work is easy or difficult. You can depend on them to be faithful all the time. The *shirkers* are always conspicuous by their absence, when there is any hard work to be done. The *jerkers* are people who are full of enthusiasm when something special is going on, but afterward they are as flat as pancakes! Enthusiasm is a God-given quality in the Holy Spirit and is characteristic of all those whose attitude to life is one of commitment.

B. Enduring Determination

"Not slothful in business . . ." (12:11, KJV). Frederick
Olford had a motto which he drilled into the lives of
his three boys: "Determination, not desire, controls our
destiny." Some people have a desire to do things, but it
gets them nowhere; they need determination to see them
through.

We find the master was characterized by this endur-
ing determination. At the outset of his ministry; yes,
even as a boy, he had a sense of vocation and calling.
When his mother Mary remonstrated with him concerning his absence from them for three days, Jesus said,
"Did you not know that I *must* be about my Father's
business?" (Luke 2:49). *There* was determination. Later
on, he declared, *"I must* work the works of him who
sent me while it is day; the night is coming when no
one can work" (John 9:4). When his disciples reasoned
with him, and Peter would have prevented his going to
the cross, he set his face determinately to go to Jerusalem
(see Luke 9:53). Is there a "must" in your life? That is
the acid test of true service.

Illustration

A twenty-three-year-old youth saw this advertisement in a
Boston newspaper: "Wanted, young man as an understudy to
a financial statistician. P. O. Box 1720." He answered the ad
but received no reply. He wrote again—no reply. A third
time—no reply. He decided to go to the post office and ask
the name of the holder of Box 1720. Refusal was given; it
was against the rules. Early one morning the young man rose
early, took the first train to Boston, went to the post office
and stood sentinel near Box 1720. After a long wait, a man
appeared, opened the box, and took out the mail. The young
man trailed him to his destination, which was the office of a
stock brokerage firm. The young man entered and asked for
the manager. When an interview was granted, he explained
how he had applied for the position several times without
receiving a response, and he went on to tell of the problem

he encountered at the post office. "But how did you find out that I was the advertiser?" queried the manager. "I stood in the lobby of the post office for several hours watching Box 1720," answered the young man. "When a man came in and took the mail from the box, I followed him here." The manager said, "Young man, you are just the kind of persistent fellow I want. You are employed!"[1]

II. Dynamic Service

". . . fervent in spirit . . ." (12:11). The word *fervent* means "boiling" or "seething." The whole idea behind the word is that we are to allow the Holy Spirit to keep us passionate and dynamic in our service all the time. Fervency is to be expressed in the realm of:

A. The Believer's Spirit

". . . fervent in spirit. . . ." The Christian temperament is compared to water boiling and bubbling over a flame; and we must always be boiling hot for God. In Revelation 3:15–16 the Lord says to the Laodicean church: "I know your works, that you are neither cold nor hot. I could wish you were cold or hot. So then, because you are lukewarm, and neither cold nor hot, I will spew you out of My mouth." He wished they were either frigid in hostility and opposition, or fervent in their love and service. This is a solemn word, and explains what we see in Christendom today. We all know of people who were once committed Christians and fervent in the work of the Lord, but they allowed their glow for Jesus Christ to cool, by neglect of communion with him and Christian fellowship and service. Such lukewarm Christians are anemic and nauseating to our Lord.

Illustration

Dr. J. H. Jowett, a famous preacher of a former generation, once confessed that his supreme difficulty during his years of training for the ministry was that of keeping his own spiritual life in warmth and vigor. Instead of being hot, on fire, we may become lukewarm or cold—spiritually slack, lazy, and undisciplined.[2]

While attending a university in London, Mahatma Gandhi became convinced that the Christian religion was the one true, supernatural religion in the world. Upon graduation, and still seeking evidence that would make him a committed Christian, Gandhi accepted employment in East Africa, living for seven months in the home of a family who were members of an evangelical Christian church. Here he felt would be the place to find the evidence he sought. But as the months passed he saw the casualness of their attitude toward the cause of God, heard them complain when they were called upon to make sacrifices for the kingdom of God and sensed their general religious apathy. Gandhi's interest turned to disappointment. "No, it is not the one true supernatural religion I had hoped to find," he said to himself. "A good religion, yes—but just one more of the many religions in the world."[3]

B. The Believer's Speech

In Acts 18:25 we read of Apollos who was ". . . fervent in spirit [and] spoke. . . ." No wonder he moved people! It is a sure sign of lukewarmness when lips are seldom opened in prayer, praise, or testimony; but when the youngest convert speaks from the heart in prayer or in testimony, however simple the language, folk will listen. Too often the outsider is put off by the person who speaks "professionally" without any sense of fervency. What the world is looking for today are people who speak with sincerity, earnestness, and fervency. It's not so much what they say as the spirit in which they say it.

Illustration

Aunt Sophie, a converted scrub woman, used to say that she was "called to scrub and preach." Wherever she went, she would tell others of Jesus, the Savior. Someone made fun of her by saying that she was seen talking about Christ to a wooden Indian, standing in front of a cigar store. When Sophie heard this, she replied, "Perhaps I did. My eyesight is not good. But talking about Christ to a wooden Indian is not so bad as being a *wooden Christian and never talking to anybody about the Lord Jesus!*" How many souls have you brought to the Lord Jesus? Are you busy telling others about the Savior?[4]

III. Devoted Service

". . . serving the Lord" (12:11). The word *serving* conveys the idea of "bondservice" or "bondslave." The apostle Paul was fond of calling himself a "bondslave." Scholars believe that the apostle took this word from the passage in Exodus 21.

When a Hebrew servant had served his master for six years, he was allowed to go free in the seventh year; but if he had come to love his master and would not leave him, a sacred ceremony was performed. He would be brought before the judges to make his decision publicly known. Then he was led to the doorpost of his master's house, and his ear lobe was bored with an awl, as an indication that he was committed to his master forever.

Our Lord considered himself a bondslave. Not only were his ears "opened" (Ps. 40:6), but he allowed his hands and feet to be nailed to a cross, because he delighted to do God's will. The bored ear of the bondslave indicated devotedness in:

A. Lowly Service

". . . he shall serve . . ." (Exod. 21:2). A slave did anything his master required of him, however lowly the service. The test of true devotedness is doing the little things. Most of us seize the opportunity to do something great and impressive, but the Lord Jesus takes cognizance of the most lowly things we do for him.

The most condescending act our Lord ever performed—outside of the cross—was when he kneeled as a
slave to wash the disciples' feet. This made such an
impression on Peter that years later he wrote in his epistle, ". . . gird up the loins of your mind, be sober . . ."
(1 Peter 1:13); or more literally, ". . . gird up the loins of
your mind with the towel of humility. . . ." Washing feet
was a slave's job; it was lowly service. So the first characteristic of a true servant is willingness to do anything.

Illustration

One day someone asked "Sophie, the scrub woman" a
question as she was scrubbing the steps of a large New
York City building. "Sophie, I understand you are a child of
God—a child of the King. Therefore, don't you think it is
beneath your level to be scrubbing these dirty steps?"
Undaunted, she replied, "There's no humiliation whatever.
You see, I'm not washing these steps for Mr. Brown, my
boss. I'm scrubbing them for Jesus Christ, my Savior!"[5]

B. Loving Service

". . . I love my master . . ." (21:5). Nothing inspires
service like love. Once you love a person you will do
anything for them. If you fall in love with Jesus Christ
you never have to be prodded into service; you can't
help but serve. When we get to that place, devoted service is as natural as breathing. We do it for sheer love
of Jesus.

Illustration

The story is told of how St. Anthony prayed and read his
Bible for hours every day, and in time became a good man.
But one day the Lord told him that there was one man better than he: Conrad, the cobbler of Jerusalem. Anthony went
to visit the cobbler to learn the secret of his goodness. Conrad remonstrated as to his goodness, but said: "If you wish
to know what I do, I don't mind telling you I mend shoes,
and I do every pair as if I were mending them for Jesus.

C. Loyal Service

". . . I will not go out free" (21:5). Many people start a job with enthusiasm, but they never see it through; their loyalty breaks down. The Lord Jesus never forces us to give our lives to him, but he expects us to do it voluntarily because we love him. Out of that love is born a loyalty.

Loyalty and teamwork in the service of the church is a wonderful thing. The church is essentially a team, and a team is built on loyalty to one another. Loyalty is fundamental to our Christian faith and service. Pray that you will always be loyal to Jesus Christ—come what may—loyal to your church, loyal to your pastor, loyal to your fellow members.

Illustration

A tourist recalls the impression made on him as he studied Poynter's great picture, "Faithful unto Death," which hung in the Walker Art Gallery in Liverpool. There stood the Roman guard on duty while the palace was falling into ruins during the destruction of Herculaneum. The dead were lying in the background, others were falling to the pavement amid the red hot eruptions of Vesuvius. Everyone who could was fleeing for his life. The Roman guard might have made his escape, but there he stood like a marble statue, preferring to remain at his post, faithful unto death. Said the tourist, "The picture has haunted me ever since. Not simply the man standing at his post of duty, but the expression of faithfulness that showed in his countenance. I have thought of it a hundred times and I have felt its influence as I have felt that of a living person."

D. Lasting Service

". . . he shall serve him forever" (21:6). At the end of his life our Savior could say, ". . . I have finished the work which you have given me to do" (John 17:4). And when Paul wrote his final letter to Timothy he said,

". . . I have finished my course, I have kept the faith" (2 Tim. 4:7, KJV).

Conclusion

You can never be devoted without being dynamic, and you will never be dynamic without being determined. Are you prepared to be a bondservant of Jesus Christ? He accepted this contract. Dare you refuse?

13

Covenant of Membership
1 Corinthians 14:36–40

"Let all things be done decently and in order"
(14:40).

Introduction

Our God is a God of order. It does not matter what passage of Scripture is turned to; whether in relation to his activities within the individual Christian or the corporate body of Christ, he is always a God of order. He is ". . . not the author of confusion but of peace . . ." (14:33).

Everyone who comes into the fellowship of an evangelical church should seriously consider the terms of membership, and then accept those terms of reference as a covenant between God and himself. It is a sad indictment on the church of Jesus Christ today that people can drift in and out of membership without anybody knowing about it; that would have never happened in New Testament times. The church of Jesus Christ, locally centered, is a family, and if an individual joins a church, whether by conversion, letter, or experience, then that person is part of the church family, and he or she can't move away without the church being painfully conscious of their absence.

Paul puts it all in the figure of a body in 1 Corinthians 12:26 where he says, ". . . if one member suffers, all the members suffer with it. . . ." God has made us that way. There is such a thing as the sympathetic system within the church of God. When someone is going through trial and tribulation, the church should seek to lift the burden and suffering of God's people. We are commanded to "Bear one another's burdens . . ." (Gal. 6:2) and, therefore, we must know the terms of our oneness and operation in Christ. These are clearly set forth in the Covenant of Membership before us. We start off, of course, with the basic fact:

> Realizing my guilt before God, I have confessed my sins to him, and received the Lord Jesus Christ, who bore my sins on the cross, as my personal Savior (see Rom. 3:19, 23; 5:8; John 1:12).

These statements concern our sinnership—the fact that Jesus died for us, and the fact that he can be received by faith into the heart and life. No one has the right to be in a local church without having experienced a conviction of sin, a conversion of life, and a confession of faith. John 1:12 says, ". . . as many as received him, to them he gave the right to become children of God, even to those who believe in his name." If I have truly received the Lord Jesus Christ into my heart and life I have a right to be in the family of God, and, therefore, in the fellowship of God.

Contrary to some teaching abroad today, my right to be in the church of Jesus Christ is not the measure of *light* I have, but the measure of *life* I have. My right to be at the Lord's table, my right to be in the local fellowship, is the fact that I share the same resurrection life of Jesus Christ that you share. My children have a right to sit at my table and eat my food, not because they know as much as Father does, but because they share my life; they are my children.

> I ACKNOWLEDGE the Lord Jesus Christ as Lord of all my life, and seek to confess him as such before others by the testimony both of life and lip (see Rom. 10:9; 2 Cor. 5:14–15).

Some religious leaders speak of the church as the final authority. The evangelical church, on the other hand, talks of Christ mediating and ministering authority through the Spirit, by the Word. To challenge the authority and sovereignty of Jesus Christ in a local church is to bring confusion into the assembly of God's people. Jesus said, ". . . Every . . . house divided against itself will not stand" (Matt. 12:25). A church can only live in revival blessing when there is the total recognition of the Lordship of Jesus Christ. We talk about the Lord's table that we recognize. We talk about the Lord's death that we celebrate. We talk about the Lord's body that we discern. We talk about the Lord's day that we observe. So his sovereignty is absolutely essential in a church where holiness and harmony are being to be enjoyed.

> I TRUST in the power of the Holy Spirit, who lives in my heart, to keep me, guide me and lead me in the way of purity and holiness (see John 14:26; 16:13; Rom. 8:2–4; Gal. 5:22–25).

The more we study the Bible and pray, the more we realize that the supreme purpose of revelation and redemption is the holiness of God's people, both individually and corporately.

Think for a moment. Why did God give us this Bible? Not that we might know all that God is like; for, ultimately, we do not have a complete revelation of him in the Bible. It isn't to have a full story of the life of Jesus Christ, for the revelation we have of him is quite fragmentary. We know nothing, for instance, of the first thirty years of his life, except for one brief glimpse at the age of 12. Practically all that is said about the Lord Jesus Christ is related to those final few weeks before he died. The Bible isn't a final statement on cosmology, anthropology, history, or poetry. Why then has it been given to us? Second Timothy 3:16–17 gives us the answer: "All Scripture is given by inspiration of God, and is profitable for doctrine, for reproof, for correction, for instruction in righteousness, that the man of God may be complete, thoroughly equipped for every good work."

The revelation of God in the Bible is to make us like Jesus, to make us perfect, to make us holy (see 1 Thess. 4:7). You ask, "Why did Jesus die?" "Why did he rise from the dead?" "Why has he become a mighty Savior?" Titus 2:11–14 tells us: "For the grace of God that brings salvation has appeared to all men, teaching us that, denying ungodliness and worldly lusts, we should live soberly, righteously, and godly in the present age, looking for the blessed hope and glorious appearing of our great God and Savior Jesus Christ, who gave himself for us, that he might redeem us from every lawless deed and purify for himself his own special people, zealous for good works." So whether it's revelation or redemption, the purpose is the same: to make us holy men and women. The whole sweep of Scripture is to bring individuals to the place of holy living. No wonder that saintly man of God, Robert Murray McCheyne (who died at the age of thirty), made this statement: "The ambition of my life is to be as holy as a saved sinner can be."

Many people think that the local church is a social club, a place to meet for dances or bazaars; but the Bible makes it clear that the reason we belong to a local church is that by the study of God's Word, by prayer, by the filling of the Holy Spirit, we might be guarded and guided in the way of holiness, fellowship, and service.

I ACCEPT the Bible as the inspired Word of God, and my
final authority in all matters of faith and practice (see 2
Tim. 3:16; 2 Peter 1:20–21).

We believe that the Scriptures were originally inspired
of God and preserved throughout the ages as the infallible rule of faith and practice. It is of first importance that
we believe that; otherwise we become the victims of
human judgment. It is not what man has to say, but what
God has to say that matters. If we make the Bible the absolute standard of faith and practice we can never go wrong.
The person who argues "Yes, but that was sufficient for
apostolic times; we have gotten beyond that" immediately
undermines the position we stand for, namely, that the
Scriptures are sufficient for all matters of faith and practice. Everything we need to know is included in this wonderful book. So constitutional requirements for pastors,
elders, deacons, deaconesses, and members, as well as all
matters of church polity and government, must conform
strictly to what the Bible has to say. Should we be unclear
on any matter, then let's table it and study the Scriptures
together until we are clear. But let the answer come from
the Word of God, for God has only promised to bless what
we do, ". . . according to the pattern . . . shown . . . on the
mountain" (Exod. 25:9, 40).

I RECOGNIZE my responsibility by tithes and offerings to
extend the kingdom of the Lord Jesus Christ both at home
and abroad (see Mal. 3:8–10; 1 Cor. 16:2; 2 Cor. 9:7).

The Bible teaches clearly that pastor and people are
responsible for tithes and offerings (see Mal. 3:8–10)—a
tithe being a tenth of my income; the offerings being over
and above the tithe. Whatever God lays on our hearts to
give should be done out of sheer love and devotion to him.
Every church should be self-supporting. The seal of
God's blessing on a local church is its ability to carry its
entire financial load. Anything less than that should be

examined and corrected. If people give in accordance with the terms of this covenant they will never lack. J. Hudson Taylor put it perfectly when he said, "God's work, done in God's way, will never lack God's supply."

> I RECOGNIZE my responsibility to pray regularly for the work of this church, for its pastors, officers and members, that the witness of all concerned may be to the glory of God and to the salvation of souls (see Eph. 6:18–19; 1 Thess. 5:17, 25).

At our weekly prayer meetings, in our own quiet times, and at our family altars with our children, we should pray for the pastors, the officers, the members, and the work of the church. This is part of our total responsibility.

Stephen Olford recalls that at his former church (Duke Street Baptist Church, Richmond, Surrey, England) the names of all the members were printed in a prayer calendar called "Prayer Requests." The names were listed alphabetically under each day of the month (31 days in a month). On the first day of the month each member would start to pray for the group in which his name occurred. The second day would be the next letter, and so on. This meant that every day everybody in the church was prayed for at least once, and those who used that prayer list morning and evening were prayed for twice. People who were serious about prayer couldn't go on praying for Mrs. Brown month after month without finding out who Mrs. Brown was! After awhile people were meeting and talking together. (Incidentally, all the addresses were given out so that members could visit each other. As a result, the fellowship became a closely knit one.)

> I RECOGNIZE my responsibility to be regular in my attendance at the services of the church, and at the Lord's table (see Acts 2:42; Heb. 10:25; 1 Cor. 11:26).

No one should join a local church and then fail to support that church by regular attendance at all official services—official services being Sunday morning, Sunday evening, Wednesday prayer meeting, and every church business meeting. Over and above that would be extra meetings, such as the missionary conference, or other similar gatherings. Attendance should not be simply to please the pastor, or to impress fellow members, but to obey and honor the Lord. Our responsibility in this regard is absolute, not relative.

In Stephen Olford's church in England, there was a dear man who regarded attendance at all services such a covenant with his Lord that he would send a letter of apology whenever he was unable to attend. It was sent either to the secretary of the church or to the pastor, and read something like this: "Dear Pastor," or "Dear Mr. Edwards, I just want to tell you that I shall not be at the prayer meeting next week. I have a commitment which has been booked for many months. I shall be very sorry to miss the blessing, but I will be with you in spirit."

Oh, for that kind of spirit today in an hour when folk shrug their shoulders and say, "So what! Who is going to involve me in such a commitment as to attend church services regularly?" Yet it has nothing to do with the pastor, or a church, but with the Lord.

I HAVE BEEN BAPTIZED by immersion, in obedience to my Lord's command, thus signifying my union with Christ in his death, burial, and resurrection (see Matt. 28:19–20; Rom. 6:4).

In the early church, there was no such person as an unbaptized believer. All who were able to be baptized were baptized. There was only one exception, and that was the thief on the cross. We are right and in accord with Scripture when we insist that before people come into membership they should show their oneness with Jesus, oneness with his people, oneness with the Word, by obeying the simple rite of baptism, and entering into the blessing. Jesus said, "If you know these things, happy are you if you do them" (John 13:17).

At this point in the instruction, potential members should be asked to indicate that they have read the Articles of Faith as contained in the by-laws, and that they are in perfect agreement with them. In the presence of the Board of Elders, the candidates must then sign their names to the Covenant, implying the ready assent of their hearts to each of the clauses, and acknowledging their dependency on the Lord to fulfill its terms. They are also encouraged to review the Covenant of Membership from time to time and reaffirm the pledge they have made to the Lord.

We have seen, then, what we mean by the Covenant of Membership—guidelines based on Scripture—so that individuals seeking to align themselves with a local church might not come in confused, perplexed, or bewildered, but rather ". . . decently and in order" (14:40). God, enable us to remember these terms, that we might be loyal, loving, and living members of the local church.

Covenant of Membership

Realizing my guilt before God, I have confessed my sins to him, and received the Lord Jesus Christ, who bore my sins on the cross, as my personal Savior (see Rom. 3:19, 23; 5:8; John 1:12).

I ACKNOWLEDGE the Lord Jesus Christ as Lord of all my life, and seek to confess him as such before others by the testimony both of life and lip (see Rom. 10:9; 2 Cor. 5:14–15).

I TRUST in the power of the Holy Spirit, who lives in my heart, to keep me, guide me, and lead me in the way of purity and holiness (see John 14:26; 16:13; Rom. 8:2–4; Gal. 5:22–25).

I ACCEPT the Bible as the inspired Word of God, and my final authority in all matters of faith and practice (see 2 Tim. 3:16; 2 Peter 1:20–21).

I RECOGNIZE my responsibility by tithes and offerings to extend the kingdom of the Lord Jesus Christ both at home and abroad (see Mal. 3:8–10; 1 Cor. 16:2; 2 Cor. 9:7).

I RECOGNIZE my responsibility to pray regularly for the work of this church, for its pastors, officers, and members, that the witness of all concerned may be to the glory of God and to the salvation of souls (see Eph. 6:18–19; 1 Thess. 5:17, 25).

I RECOGNIZE my responsibility to be regular in my attendance at the services of the church, and at the Lord's table (see Acts 2:42; Heb. 10:25; 1 Cor. 11:26).

I HAVE BEEN BAPTIZED BY IMMERSION, in obedience to my Lord's command, thus signifying my union with Christ in his death, burial, and resurrection (see Matt. 28:19–20; Rom. 6:4).

I HAVE READ the Articles of Faith as contained in the by-laws and am in complete agreement therewith (see 1 Tim. 6:12; 2 Tim. 4:7; Jude 3).

Recognizing my inability in my own strength to adhere to the terms of any covenant, yet believing that my Lord will enable me to fulfill the terms of this Covenant, I hereby attach my signature below, implying the ready assent of my heart to each of the above clauses (see Phil. 4:13).

Signature _____

Date _____

Witness (Pastor) _____

Articles of Faith

We believe in one God, eternally existent as God the Father, God the Son, and God the Holy Spirit.

We believe that the Bible, composed of the Old and New Testaments, is God's inspired and infallible Word, and is the supreme standard and final authority for all conduct, faith, and doctrine.

We believe in the deity of the Lord Jesus Christ, in his virgin birth, in his sinless life, in his miracles, in his vicarious and atoning death, in his bodily resurrection, in his ascension to the right hand of the Father, and in his premillenial, personal return in power and glory.

We believe that man was created in the image of God, but by willful transgression became sinful and is justly under the condemnation and wrath of Almighty God.

We believe that the only salvation from this guilt and condemnation is through faith in the righteousness and atonement of the Lord Jesus Christ, and that this salvation is the free gift of God's love and grace.

We believe in the personality of the Holy Spirit and that his ministry is to reveal Christ to men, to convict of sin, to regenerate repentant sinners and, by his presence and power, to sanctify the lives of the redeemed.

We believe that the Lord Jesus Christ instituted the ordinances of baptism and communion; that baptism is only to be administered upon profession of faith in Christ, by immersion, thereby declaring our faith in a crucified, buried, and risen Savior; that communion is only for believers, is to be preceded by faithful self-examination, and is in remembrance of the Lord's death until he comes.

We believe that a New Testament church is a body of believers, baptized by immersion, associated for worship, service, and the spread of the gospel of the grace of God to all the world.

We believe that there will be a resurrection of the just and the unjust; the just, having been redeemed by the shed blood of the Lord Jesus Christ, to be with him throughout eternity in glory; the unjust, having died impenitent and unreconciled to God, to eternal condemnation in hell.

Endnotes

Chapter 1

1. *Sunday School Times*, quoted in Walter B. Knight, *Knight's Master Book of New Illustrations* (Grand Rapids: Eerdmans, 1956), p. 638, adapted.

2. A. Naismith, *1,200 Notes, Quotes, and Anecdotes* (Hammersmith: Pickering & Inglis, 1963), p. 55.

3. Knight, *Knight's Master Book of New Illustrations*, p. 139.

4. *New Illustrator*, quoted in Walter B. Knight, *3,000 Illustrations for Christian Service* (Grand Rapids: Eerdmans, 1952), p. 431, adapted.

5. *The King's Business*, ibid., 427, adapted.

Chapter 2

1. A. Naismith, *1,200 Notes, Quotes, and Anecdotes* (Hammersmith: Pickering & Inglis, 1963), p. 197.

2. T. T. Shields, *The Gospel Witness.*

3. Henry G. Weston.

4. *Gospel Herald*, quoted in Walter B. Knight, *3,000 Illustrations for Christian Service* (Grand Rapids: Eerdmans, 1952), p. 296, adapted.

Chapter 3

1. V. Raymond Edman, "The Discipline of Discipleship" in *The Disciplines of Life* (Wheaton, Ill.: Scripture Press, 1948), pp. 12–13.

2. Dietrich Bonhoeffer, *Life Together* (New York: Harper and Brothers, 1954), p. 8.

3. See Leon Morris, *The Gospel According to St. Luke,* Tyndale New Testament Commentaries (Grand Rapids: Eerdmans, 1960), p. 180.

4. H. G. Bosch, *Our Daily Bread* (Grand Rapids: Radio Bible Class, n.d.).

5. David Brown, *Commentary on the Old and New Testaments*, vol. 5 (Chicago: Moody Press, 1945), p. 56.

Chapter 4

1. Albert Mygatt, quoted in Paul Lee Tan, *Encyclopedia of 7,700 Illustrations* (Garland, Tex.: Bible Communications, 1979), p. 541.

2. James C. Hefley, ibid., 757.

3. John Wesley, quoted in *Christian History,* vol. II, no. 1.

Chapter 5

1. *Gospel Herald*, quoted in Walter B. Knight, *3,000 Illustrations for Christian Service* (Grand Rapids: Eerdmans, 1952), pp. 516–17.

2. A. J. Gordon, quoted in Walter B. Knight, *Knight's Master Book of New Illustrations* (Grand Rapids: Eerdmans, 1956), pp. 288–89.

Chapter 6

1. *Our Daily Bread* (Grand Rapids: Radio Bible Class, n.d.), adapted.

Chapter 7

1. Jesse B. Deloe, *Sweeter Than Honey* (BMH, 1979), p. 151.

2. H. G. Bosch, *Our Daily Bread* (Grand Rapids: Radio Bible Class, Sept. 20, 1972).

3. Amos R. Wells, *Pulpit Helps* (Chattanooga, Tenn.: AMG International).

Chapter 8

1. John Stott, *Baptism and Fullness: The Work of the Holy Spirit Today* (Downers Grove, Ill.: InterVarsity Press, 1976), p. 16.

2. *Leadership* (Fall 1985), p. 76.

3. *Drastic Discipleship* (Grand Rapids), adapted.

4. *Choice Gleanings* (Grand Rapids: Gospel Folio Press, Dec. 6, 1978).

5. R. W. DeHaan, *Our Daily Bread* (Grand Rapids: Radio Bible Class), adapted.

Chapter 9

1. Howard G. Hendricks, *Say It With Love* (Wheaton, Ill.: Victor Books, 1972), p. 49, adapted.

Chapter 10

1. Paul Lee Tan, *Encyclopedia of 7,700 Illustrations* (Garland, Tex.: Bible Communications, 1979), p. 763, adapted.

2. Paul S. Rees, ibid., 271.

3. *Leadership* (Fall 1983), p. 87.

4. Copyright 1914 by Charles H. Gabriel. © renewed 1942 by The Rodeheaver Company. All rights reserved. Used by permission.

Chapter 11

1. *Now,* quoted in Walter B. Knight, *Knight's Master Book of New Illustrations* (Grand Rapids: Eerdmans, 1956), p. 244, adapted.

2. *Christianity Today,* quoted in Paul Lee Tan, *Encyclopedia of 7,700 Illustrations* (Garland, Tex.: Bible Communications, 1979), p. 1353.

Chapter 12

1. *Sunshine Magazine,* quoted in Paul Lee Tan, *Encyclopedia of 7,700 Illustrations* (Garland, Tex.: Bible Communications, 1979), p. 1672.

2. Derek J. Prime, "Aglow With the Spirit," *Christian Irishman* (Belfast, North Ireland, June, 1985), p. 8.

3. Tan, *Encyclopedia of 7,700 Illustrations*, pp. 765–66.

4. *Gospel Herald*, quoted in Walter B. Knight, *Knight's Master Book of New Illustrations* (Grand Rapids: Eerdmans, 1956), p. 649.

5. Ibid., 746.

For Further Reading

Barclay, William. *Daily Study Bible* (1 Corinthians). Rev. ed. Philadelphia: Westminster Press, 1975–1976.

_____. *Daily Study Bible* (Matthew). Rev. ed. Philadelphia: Westminster Press, 1975–1976.

_____. *Daily Study Bible* (Romans). Rev. ed. Philadelphia: Westminster Press, 1975–1976.

Barnhouse, Donald Grey. *Exposition of Bible Doctrines: Taking the Epistle to the Romans as a Point of Departure.* 10 vols. Grand Rapids: Wm. B. Eerdmans Publishing Co., 1952–1963.

Bonhoeffer, Dietrich. *The Cost of Discipleship.* New York: Macmillan Publishing Co., Inc., 1963.

Briscoe, D. Stuart. *The Communicator's Commentary* (Romans). Vol. 6. Waco, Tex.: Word Inc., 1982.

Bruce, F. F. *The Letter of Paul to the Romans.* Rev. ed. Tyndale New Testament Commentaries. Grand Rapids: Wm. B. Eerdmans Publishing Co., 1985.

Bush, George. *Notes on Exodus.* 2 vols. in 1. Minneapolis: Klock and Klock Publishing Co., 1976.

Craigie, P. C. *New International Commentary on the Old Testament.* Grand Rapids: Wm. B. Eerdmans Publishing Co., 1976.

Edwards, Thomas Charles. *A Commentary on the First Epistle to the Corinthians.* 2nd ed. London: Hodder and Stoughton, 1885.

Getz, Gene A. *A Biblical Theology of Material Possessions.* Chicago: Moody Press, 1990.

Godet, F. *Commentary on First Corinthians.* Grand Rapids: Kregel Publications, 1977.

Haldane, Robert. *Exposition of the Epistles to the Romans.* Evansville, Ind.: The Sovereign Grace Book Club, 1958.

Hanks, Billie, Jr., and William A. Shell, eds. *Discipleship.* Grand Rapids: Zondervan Publishing House, 1981.

Henrichsen, Walter A. *Disciples Are Made—not Born.* Wheaton, Ill.: Victor Books.

Hobbs, Herschel. *The Epistles to the Corinthians.* Grand Rapids: Baker Book House, 1960.

Hodge, Charles. *An Exposition of the Second Epistle to the Corinthians.* Grand Rapids: Baker Book House, 1980.

Ironside, H. A. *First Epistle to the Corinthians.* Neptune, N.J.: Loizeaux Brothers, Inc.

_____. *Lectures on the Epistle to the Romans.* Neptune, N.J.: Loizeaux Brothers, Inc., 1962.

Johnson, Alan F. *The Freedom Letter.* 2 vols. Chicago: Moody Press, 1985.

Law, Henry. *Christ Is All: The Gospel of the Pentateuch.* 4 vols. 1867. Vols 1 (*The Gospel in Genesis*) and 2 (*The Gospel in Exodus*). Reprint. London: Banner of Truth Trust, 1967.

Lloyd-Jones, D. Martyn. *Romans: An Exposition.* Grand Rapids: Zondervan Publishing House, 1971.

Luther, Martin. *Commentary on the Epistle of Romans.* Grand Rapids: Zondervan Publishing House, 1960.

Mackintosh, Charles Henry. *Genesis to Deuteronomy: Notes on the Pentateuch.* 6 vols. 1880–1882. Reprint ed. 1 vol. Neptune, N.J.: Loizeaux Brothers, Inc., 1972.

Meyer, F. B. *The Christ-Life for the Self-Life.* Chicago: Moody Press, n.d.

_____. *Devotional Commentary* (Exodus). London: Marshall, Morgan & Scott, 1952.

Morgan, G. Campbell. *The Corinthian Letters of Paul: An Exposition of I and II Corinthians.* Westwood, N.J.: Fleming H. Revell, 1946.

_____. *Discipleship.* London: Allenson & Co. Ltd., 1934.

_____. *The Gospel According to Matthew.* New York: Fleming H. Revell Co., 1929.

Morris, Leon. *The First Epistle of Paul to the Corinthians.* Tyndale New Testament Commentaries. Grand Rapids: Wm. B. Eerdmans Publishing Co., 1958.

Moule, Handley C. G. *The Epistle of St. Paul to the Romans.* Minneapolis: Klock and Klock Christian Publishers, 1982.

Moule, Handley. *The Second Epistle to the Corinthians: A Translation, Paraphrase, and Exposition.* Ed. A. W. Handley Moule. London: Pickering & Inglis, 1962.

Murphy, James Gracey. *A Critical and Exegetical Commentary on the Book of Exodus.* Minneapolis: Klock and Klock Christian Publishers, 1980.

Newell, William R. *Romans Verse by Verse.* Chicago: Moody Press, 1938.

Olford, Stephen F. *The Grace of Giving.* Rev. ed. Memphis: Encounter Ministries, Inc., 1990.

Ortiz, Juan Carlos. *Disciple.* Carol Stream, Ill.: Creation House, 1975.

Phillips, John. *Exploring Romans.* Chicago: Moody Press, 1969.

Rendall, T. S. *Discipleship in Depth: What It Means to Be Christ's Disciple in the Space Age.* Three Hills, Alberta, Canada: Prairie Press, 1981.

Schultz, Samuel J. *The Old Testament Speaks.* New York: Harper Brothers, 1960.

Spurgeon, C. H. *The Gospel of the Kingdom.* Grand Rapids: Zondervan Publishing House, 1962.

Stifler, James M. *The Epistle to the Romans.* Chicago: Moody Press, 1960.

Sugden, Christopher. *Radical Discipleship.* London: Marshall, Morgan & Scott, 1981.

Tasker, R. V. G. *The Gospel According to St. Matthew.* Tyndale New Testament Commentaries. Grand Rapids: Wm. B. Eerdmans Publishing Co., 1961.

Thomas, W. H. Griffith. *St. Paul's Epistle to the Romans. A Devotional Commentary.* Grand Rapids: Wm. B. Eerdmans Publishing Co., 1946.

Verwer, George. *No Turning Back.* Wheaton, Ill.: Tyndale House Publishers, Inc., 1983.

Vine, W. E. *I Corinthians.* Grand Rapids: Zondervan Publishing House, 1961.

Walvoord, John F. *Matthew: Thy Kingdom Come.* Chicago: Moody Press, 1974.

Watson, David. *Called and Committed: World-Changing Discipleship.* Wheaton, Ill.: Harold Shaw Publishers, 1982.

_____. *Discipleship.* Copyright 1981 by Shalom Trust. London: Hodder and Stoughton, Ltd., 1983.

Wiersbe, Warren W. *Be Right* (Romans). Wheaton, Ill.: Scripture Press, 1977.